BRANDING FOR BUYOUT

How to Tell Your Story and Get the Deal You Deserve

BRANDING FOR BUYOUT

How to Tell Your Story and Get the Deal You Deserve

TED SCHLUETER

THE Grist

Grist Mill Books, a subsidiary of The Grist, Inc.
125 High Street, 3rd Floor
Boston, MA 02110

For information about special discounts on bulk purchases for
promotional, educational, or business use, as well as author
appearances, please contact the business development team
at Branding For Buyout: 617-390-8958 or
PR@brandingforbuyout.com

Printed in the United States of America
Illustrations and Book Design by The Grist

Library of Congress Control Number: 2021910828

For Teddy and Sophie

Always believe in yourselves

Contents

Thus, the task is not so much to see what no one yet has seen, but to think what nobody yet has thought about that which everybody sees.

Arthur Schopenhauer

Introduction: How Can You Realize Your Vision?

You're an entrepreneur who has spent a lot of time building something—something worth a lot to you and to your employees. You probably built it with your own hands, at enormous personal sacrifice. You've felt a lot of pain. Occasional joy. Fleeting moments of pride. This thing you built is probably 80 or 90 percent of your net worth—so you want to get the most value out of it that you can. But you have absolutely no idea how to sell it, and that scares the hell out of you. And you aren't looking for someone to tell you what you already know about the business you built—or to hand the process off to a banker to run a color-by-numbers process just driven by the math. You're an entrepreneur. You want to transform your business into the full glory of what you envisioned. You want to see the grain you harvested in the field ground up into the magic of flour and unlimited possibilities. You want exponential value. Am I speaking your language? Keep reading.

Why do you do it?

Why do you invest your time, energy, passion, and labor trying to make your company—*your thing*—a success?

Sure, there are the elements of pride and satisfaction that come from winning, however you define them.

But for most of us, the reason we do it is to create value. It's to build something that produces revenue and can grow until it's eventually time to do the next thing. The effort translates into an exit—which, for the purposes of this book, means getting bought by a strategic acquirer. But you'll find that running the playbook successfully is effective for other "partial" exits, too, from selling a chunk of equity to outside investors or going through the process of an initial public offering and selling stock. In all those cases, the branding skills we'll be discussing will reveal value that translates into a more desirable outcome.

If you're an entrepreneur, you've done a lot of the hard parts. You had the idea. You built a framework. You have systems in place to handle the day-to-day. You're watching the metrics that matter most for keeping your business alive and (hopefully) thriving. You're used to the pressures that come with keeping the lights on and the doors open.

There are lots of experts out there who can tell you how to find the right accountant, or get on the best platform for selling your product or service, or make the right hire for that open IT or regional sales position.

That's not why I'm here.

I'm an entrepreneur, just like you. I share all those same

concerns. I'm here because I don't want to see you put in all the time, energy, passion, and labor in and end up with less than you deserve when it's time to sell. I had it happen to me personally earlier in my career, when I had the opportunity to sell my first business out from under the umbrella of another organization. I didn't have as much control over the process —as I expected, and the entire experience was a collection of "if-I-had-only-knowns." That personal experience drove me to improve the process not only for myself, but to figure out ways for clients to intentionally engineer a process that reveals everything their brand was worth. My track record over the last 15 years proves this works.

The cases you're going to read about here will show you exactly what I mean. I've helped entrepreneurs position brands to be acquired by global powerhouses in packaged foods (PepsiCo), consumer goods (3M), apparel (Lotto Sport Italia), and B-to-B technology (Snow), among other categories. These entrepreneurs not only lived to tell the story, but also found substantially better returns than if they had just sat back and "trusted" the process.

Through those cases and the analysis that comes with them, I'm going to show you the steps you can take right now to engineer that better exit for yourself. You can take more control over your brand and a potential exit—long before it actually happens. You'll learn how to show a potential buyer not just what you are today, but what your brand could look like in the future if placed in the right hands.

I'm not talking about financial alchemy, either—polishing

the numbers so they look better on a spreadsheet or in a PowerPoint deck. That's a standard part of deal-making, like making sure your house is clean for the next showing by your realtor.

This book and the methodology in it are tools you will use to prepare your brand for an exit. I realize that "brand" is both an overused and misunderstood term. Some entrepreneurs use it interchangeably with the product or service or technology they're selling. Others sneer at the term and think it's something a marketer made up to justify attaching more budget to a "campaign." But I'm here to tell you—and I'll prove to you through the case studies in this book—that when you do concrete, measurable work on your brand, it will show up in real dollars at the deal closing.

It's true no matter what business category you're in, and no matter what the current economic conditions are. You have options and strategies you can use to make your brand stronger and more attractive to an array of buyers—from ones who are looking to add you to a strategic portfolio they already own, to others that are looking at it as strictly a financial play. We'll even cover situations where the buyer is motivated almost purely by emotion.

There is a better way to tell your brand story, and to provide the powerful context that makes that story resonate with potential energy. A way that isn't just an automatic process, dominated by bankers and lawyers trying to close a deal as quickly as they can so they can move on to the next one.

Complex deals require expertise from investment bankers,

accountants, and lawyers, for sure. But that doesn't mean that you—or your brand—should give up a seat at the table. I'll show you how to make sure you have that space to tell your story.

What is Branding For Buyout?

Simply put, Branding For Buyout is designed to tell your story in a way a set of dry financials or a lackluster CIM (Confidential Investment Memorandum) can't. Using a series of case studies from clients and colleagues—and plenty of the wins and losses I've experienced myself along the way—I'm going to show you how to better understand exactly what you have, how to keep your eyes open for potential acquirers, and how to understand what all the different players at the deal table—the potential acquirers, investment bankers, lawyers, and accountants—are supposed to do. And I'll back it up with real-world examples, data, and post-deal analysis from the principals involved.

By demystifying the branding and exit processes, I'll help you focus your energy on the decisions that will provide quantifiable value. You'll be less likely to make a mistake out of panic, fear, or incomplete information. Ask any entrepreneur who's been through an exit and he or she will tell you that experiencing one is the best preparation. It's like driving at night with no headlights—not to mention that it can take your focus away from running your business day-to-day.

By telling these stories, pulling back the curtain on some of the unknowns, and sharing this advice, I'm going to help you shorten the learning curve and take away some of the stress and fear that almost automatically come with such a meaningful and high-stakes transaction. That's just as true if you're doing this for the first time or if you're an entrepreneur who's been through it once and wants a more comprehensive playbook for the next go-round.

While there are entire university modules, squadrons of advisors, stacks and stacks of books, and long lists of seminars out there to show you how to get *in* as an entrepreneur—from generating concepts to finding funding—and how to scale your business, there's almost nothing to help the entrepreneur who is ready to *get out and do* this kind of work.

That's where Branding For Buyout comes in.

Who will need this book?

The world is full of what investment bankers call "lower middle-market" entrepreneurs—people just like you who have built promising and successful businesses that have sales of $5 million to $150 million. We're talking about anything from a cutting-edge B-to-B tech company to a growing chain of regional restaurants to a custom clothing brand to a partnership that has created the trendiest new smart gadget.

Any new MBA grad can tell you about the basic fundamentals of a publicly traded company from its stock trends and trail of financial disclosures. But when you get to private or emerging or more niche businesses, there is far less public information (or none!)—and what information *is* disclosed isn't regulated like that of public companies. A lot of it is one-sided and subjective, or deeply speculative about the future of a segment or an entire emerging industry.

Given those treacherous waters, it isn't shocking that companies looking to acquire in that environment come in with shields up. If you're selling, you may have a mountain to climb. As the person fully invested in the day-to-day and potential of your business, you know it better than anyone. But few (if any!) other people know that story. Plus, you could well be dealing with potential acquirers who come into a transaction with far more deal-making experience than you, and with far more resources. They have more attorneys, more accountants, more time, and less emotional investment in the game that is about to be played. They have a significant strategic advantage.

So what do you do about that?

How do you know what you really have? How do you know who might be interested in it? How can you best tell the story of your brand and make a deal that produces a win for everyone at the table? Where do you go to find the expert consultants you need? If you're looking for the answers to those questions, Branding For Buyout is for you.

The average exit "process" for an entrepreneur selling his or her business takes between 18 to 24 months from concept to closing, with about six months of that dedicated to engineering a specific deal with the ultimate acquirer. It's an exhausting gauntlet of soul-searching, meeting, consulting, decision-making, strategizing, and second-guessing. Plenty of entrepreneurs operate from a position of weakness and take the first deal they're offered. Those in a more select group get skilled guidance from a mentor or an investment banker, and at least have the financial and operational lives of the business organized and prepared for the scrutiny of a sale. But very few entrepreneurs do the specific work on their brand *before the dating game even starts* that can translate into an even stronger sales multiple (meaning a profit many times the amount of the original value). Very few are moving beyond relying on the CIM created by an investment banker and pitching their brand across every touchpoint for both the customer and the potential acquirer—and successfully telling the story not just of what they are but what they could be.

Tech giants like Facebook understand this dynamic. Facebook paid $1 billion for Instagram in 2012 not because Instagram was making huge revenues (it didn't have any) or bringing an army of operational talent to the table (it had only 13 employees). Instagram's brand was powerful in the space where Facebook wanted to be, and Instagram told a powerful story over the course of a two-year courtship.

On a more "real world" scale, Etonic was a brand with more than 100 years of history and tradition in the footwear business, but by the early 2000s it had become known more for being the bottom-dollar golf shoe in every discount store you've ever seen. After a group of Boston-area private investors bought the brand from Spalding in 2003, I helped them resuscitate the brand's iconic American heritage while highlighting the tech-forward innovations across multiple sports: golf, running, walking, and bowling. In three years, the investors sold Etonic to Lotto Sport Italia at a big multiple—a story you'll hear more about in Chapter 3.

In Chapter 6, you'll read about how sharpening the brand story and streamlining messaging on the packaging transformed PopCorners from a regional player in the better-for-you salty snack category into the fastest-growing brand in that category—and a priority acquisition for PepsiCo.

Are you sitting on a billion-dollar idea? Is a multinational fashion brand, a European software developer, a consumer packaged-goods giant, or an equity-backed holding company looking to buy you out? Maybe, maybe not. Whether you're a future Elon Musk or a recent college grad still in the brand new build-out phase of your big idea, the skills and strategies you need are available for you to learn in this book.

Why should you listen to me?

Helping entrepreneurs build their brands—and reveal real, tangible value—is what I do every day at The Grist, the branding and marketing company I own and operate in Boston. I've been doing this work for almost 30 years, thriving in the business-to-business and consumer spaces with brands ranging from tech to finance to apparel to consumer packaged goods. I've helped multiple companies go through the Branding For Buyout methodology and on to successful, high-multiple exits.

Of course, it's never been easier to put up a website, start some social media accounts, and call yourself an expert in something. My proof is in the case studies you'll be reading about in the chapters to come, and in the emergence and acceptance of this concept in the academic space. I've been working with my friends at Babson College and their legendary entrepreneurship program to study, systematize, and teach Branding For Buyout to emerging entrepreneurs, so they can use these necessary skills to engineer better exit outcomes right from the start. Having a brand that is attractive to both potential customers and potential investors and acquirers is already established.

Another important motivation for writing this book is that I've had to learn how to map these processes the hard way—both through experiences I've had with clients, and what I've gone through as the principal in my own companies. I've been a part of acquisitions that flourished, and ones that define buyer's remorse. I've had situations where I've done my job *too well*—where an acquiring company was so happy with the brand they bought that they got rid of me and my department, because they didn't think they needed to do any more work on it.

Mostly, I haven't just been where you sit, I'm still sitting there, right now. I know the excitement and the worry and the stress and the pain that go with being an entrepreneur. Being the person who has to keep the lights on and make payroll, I know the toll it can take on your financial and personal lives, and the challenges it places in front of you every day.

I know that when you have a story you can tell about *your thing,* you have to make the most of your opportunity. That reality is why I've chosen to build this book through real case studies, real data, and the actual stories of clients, mentors, and peers—so that they can reinforce the lessons I'm hoping to give you, and to deliver a sort of best-practices manual any of us would have loved to see ahead of our first exit. It'll free you up to become not just an entrepreneur, but a serial entrepreneur—one who wins the deal and uses the win to move on to a bigger and more rewarding challenge.

By the end of this book, I will prove to you that intentional work on your brand can not only reveal more of that brand's current value but also create new value. I'll show you how you can control your brand's story—and how it's perceived—in a way that's at least as powerful as the other tools an investment banker would use to help close the sale.

Think about it. You've devoted thousands and thousands of hours to building your business. You've probably sacrificed time with your family and friends. You've put money, heart, and soul into it. You took the risks. You took the bullets. Like Teddy Roosevelt said in his famous speech at the Sorbonne, in 1923, "the credit belongs to the man [or woman] who is actually in the arena...who at the best knows in the end the triumph of high achievement, and who at the worst, if he [she] fails, at least fails while daring greatly."

Getting this far is a big deal, and it is my mission and my passion to help you, the entrepreneur who has built something amazing to cut through the confusion and stress, realize your vision, and receive the return you deserve. All you have to do is read the book, pick up the tools, and apply the concepts to your situation. Let me show you how.

CHAPTER 1

The Epiphany: What Really Adds Value?

We had cold-called our way into BrassRing and gotten a shot at our biggest client. It was B-to-B tech in the talent-management space, which we knew little to nothing about—I know now, that's a competitive advantage. Eyes wide open, no rules, no jargon, NOT going to do whatever everyone else is doing. It was a nine-month, all-out sprint to reposition and launch a brand from the ground up, which we did. The new BrassRing brand was completely different, unique, and successful in the market. Then BrassRing was bought by Kenexa for $115 million—and I was out of a job. Wait, what?

The early 2000s were a new and booming time in digital employment management. You may remember the massive ad campaigns Monster.com ran, everywhere from daytime television to the Super Bowl. The "When I Grow Up" commercial done by Boston's Mullen (now MullenLowe) is now a classic, shot in black-and-white and featuring kids waxing poetic about how they wanted to grow up to hit the glass ceiling, work in middle management, and develop a brown nose. Whatever attention Monster wasn't getting was likely to be attracted by CareerBuilder.com, which got infusions of cash and traffic when Microsoft acquired a piece of it and made it the jobs hub on its web portal.

BrassRing was one of the first companies to enter the corporate talent-management space, in 1999, but even with investments from *The Washington Post* and venture capital, it was still a small player—doing about a million in revenue. How could it define itself as something different and special, relative to competitors like Monster and CareerBuilder—and dozens of other more specialized recruiting solutions like Taleo and Recruitmax, which were filling up the now-borderless digital space?

It started with a story.

BrassRing hired my company to expand its consulting business. We began by helping BrassRing define exactly what it was—why satisfied customers chose BrassRing, and why those who chose competitors didn't. We did a 360-degree review of the business, from both internal and external perspectives. The company's financials would tell a casual observer a very specific, limited story. What we were after was to find the fundamental selling proposition—the *why*—and make sure everything about the brand agreed with it.

It's easy enough to hire a team of graphic designers, redo a logo, and come up with a memorable phrase for a campaign. But to have value—something an investor would want to be a part of, or an acquirer would want to buy—you need to find the chord that not only makes the emotional connection but also gives a vision of what the brand could grow into and be.

I can already hear what you're saying. "What does that do for me, Ted? I make enterprise software for county tax assessors," or "I produce specialized pool-cleaning chemicals," or insert your unglamorous, supposedly non-emotional product or service here. But every business has a chance to make an emotional connection with a potential customer, because the best businesses specialize in taking away pain points and making things easy.

What were the pain points in corporate talent management? Human-resources executives and managers have these really hard—and really diverse—jobs to fill. They have to find qualified candidates for positions throughout the company who have the skills and experience necessary for the work, and fit into the company's culture. Human Resources also has to build and organize processes for onboarding, training and retention, diversity and inclusion, advancement, discipline, and employee exit.

We interviewed dozens of C-level human resources executives, who showed us that the talent-management industry as a whole was difficult. Software and technology were expensive, and so complicated that companies couldn't easily change providers. Executives tended to either avoid the segment altogether because of its complexity, or ask for an easy-to-understand service portal that could help them solve problems as they came up, and allow them to pay for the services they actually used—not add-ons that they never opened.

In those days before the cloud made coding and sharing solutions much easier, clients like Liberty Mutual and EMC chose BrassRing because the company had the technological know-how to thoroughly customize things like regulatory compliance. BrassRing would then adapt those solutions and sell them to other companies, which had related problems they wanted to solve.

Our review revealed that BrassRing set itself apart in the way it helped executives make sophisticated hires—for positions that required a nuanced set of skills and experience. You could go to a bargain-level, one-stop-shop like Monster to find somebody to work in the warehouse. BrassRing wasn't (and shouldn't be) competing in that space. But what if you needed somebody with very specific skills for a complicated job, and you needed the job filled right away?

Gary Cormier was the executive vice president of human resources at BrassRing, and he describes what happened. "I closed a deal with Sepracor, which was then the parent company that produced the sleep aid Lunesta. They needed to hire 400 sales reps who were comfortable in that product space, and they needed to do it in 30 days. They outsourced that whole business to us, because we had proven we could solve that problem."

Anecdotes like that were the basis for creating BrassRing's brand story—a platform for custom solutions. Actually, "platform" wasn't even part of the language of branding in those days, but what we did with BrassRing gave it some traction. The term comes from computing, where the platform—MacOS, Windows, Linux—is the base from which you perform all the operations you need.

BrassRing's platform was "We can diagnose exactly what kind of talent-management problem you have, and give you a customized solution"—whether it was offering technology in the form of software, consulting to help in-house processes, or operating as the conduit for outsourcing HR functions.

Building a Platform

What does branding the "how" look like? I created the description "Workforce by Design," and illustrated how BrassRing could solve a customer's problems across a variety of channels—in tech, consulting, and outsourcing.

In the 1990s *The Washington Post* and other newspapers had started to discover, painfully, that anybody could upload instantly updatable job listings that let job seekers apply directly to companies that were hiring. BrassRing needed some differentiating brand story—and a truly disruptive way to solve staffing problems at scale—or it would drown.

"When you're selling HR, you're selling a relationship," says Cormier, who came up through the world of human resources at Lotus and then IBM after its acquisition. "It isn't like selling information technology, where the tech itself is in the forefront. You're selling trust. So the brand identity had to get right to that relationship."

We told how BrassRing could cut through the clutter of hiring and recruiting in this chaotic, web-based space. Our theme became "Follow Our Lead."

The visuals were simple—a veteran New York City cab driver, showing you that the best route from midtown to JFK at rush hour wasn't the obvious straight line, but the most efficient path that came from a lifetime of experience.

That campaign put a finger on the exact pain point so many C-level executives had with staffing and recruitment—and all of them based in New York City knew the pain of getting the wrong cabbie for that rush-hour airport run.

BrassRing would represent expert guidance, a trusted resource, and an instant solution to any problem, no matter how complex. Being a reliable guide was such a killer concept because it projected leadership in the recruiting space, without making any claims to be the biggest or the most profitable company—which BrassRing wasn't!

"This original branding work wasn't so much for an exit but for leadership," says BrassRing's CEO Deb Besemer, who knew about the importance of getting a brand to the front of the pack from her time as the head of worldwide field operations for Lotus. "How do we brand ourselves appropriately for what we do—and for the effort we put in? 'Follow Our Lead' meant we were global, compliant, and reliable. Those are the things big companies and big clients care about."

To this day, BrassRing still uses the Workforce by Design platform we helped design. It was an immediate hit in three hugely important ways. In the marketplace, it was reflected by BrassRing moving to No. 1 in its category, securing huge clients like IKEA, Nissan, BMW, and Time Warner. The company's status and position in the industry changed, too. It won consecutive Codie Awards from the Software & Information Industry Association for best human resources product. It even helped BrassRing orient itself internally. Says Besemer, "It wove our internal processes together, and made it clear to everybody in the organization what we were specifically about—getting the workforce that works for you through technology, consulting, and outsourcing."

BrassRing's revenue went from $1 million to $40 million, and the scale of that success and the authority the brand had in its space brought an unintended consequence. It made the company a target for early acquisition. Kenexa was a large human-capital management group that wasn't a direct competitor to BrassRing, but wanted to move upmarket into that space. "Our brand in the market was as recruiting experts for large companies. That's everything Kenexa wanted," says Besemer. "They wanted to go upmarket, and buying us gave them permission to go after those clients."

Kenexa bought BrassRing for $115 million in 2005, but didn't stop there. By aggregating BrassRing's expertise with its other human-resources assets, Kenexa grew its business with even more diverse platforms. That caught IBM's eye, and IBM bought Kenexa for $1.2 billion in 2012.

When the deal closed, BrassRing brought everybody together to share the news, and the executive team was understandably thrilled (and, in some cases, more than a little richer!). I got my share of handshakes, high-fives, and pats on the back, and Deb, Gary, and the rest of the executive team made it clear how valuable my company's work was in showing BrassRing's value to Kenexa. I was excited to hear what came next—hopefully, bigger and better projects with BrassRing and its new corporate parent.

But there was no next. Kenexa was a big company, and it had its own marketing team. My contract didn't make the transition, and it was over.

It was a shock, to be honest. I had designed the branding plays, but BrassRing was the one running the playbook.

My first reaction was, "I don't want that to ever happen to me again."

Then I had an epiphany: "Wait a second. What happened with BrassRing *could* happen again."

There are hundreds, no, thousands of companies out there

that are in some stage of the sale process. An entrepreneur is considering selling his or her life's work to a bigger company that can take it and run with it. A company has already sold a chunk of itself to a venture-capital firm as a form of financing, and now the leaders want to get all the way out. A small, boutique company comes up with a world-changing product and is being chased by all the big boys. You name the scenario, and it's out there.

Accountants have a handle on the numbers. Lawyers are there to keep track of the details. Investment bankers know the marketplace and how to sell the deal. So, good financials, a record of excellent compliance, and a sophisticated and polished printed summary of the business can translate into strong interest from a buyer and the chance to make a successful exit. But what about the brand?

If you can learn how to tell your brand story better, you can reveal more intrinsic value than other companies anxious for a buyout. You can open the sale up to potential buyers and markets that you might not have ever considered. You can build your brand so that every touchpoint is calibrated for a potential sale—not just a talking point on the sales-funnel page of your website.

BrassRing is the perfect example. In 2004 it would have been regarded as old media desperately trying to keep a piece of the classified-ad business (in other words, a fancy job board). Because BrassRing didn't have a clear mission and a strong brand, one of the big players like Monster could well have come in, offered the $40/$50 million *The Washington Post* and a venture-capital group had in the deal, and BrassRing would probably have been content to escape without any losses.

But by clearly delineating the brand and staking out fresh space in the market—which we're going to talk a lot more about in Chapter 3—BrassRing improved the business in terms of raw sales numbers and revenue, and increased the value of the brand.

I can compare this to a sports story. Bob Kraft bought the New England Patriots for $172 million in 1994—the highest price ever paid for an NFL team at the time. Since then, he's done a lot with the brand. He hired Bill Belichick as the coach, drafted Tom Brady to play quarterback, and built his own, mostly-privately-funded stadium, and the team has won six Super Bowls. Regardless of what the Patriots' financials look like since the pandemic (or the fact that Tom Brady moved on to the Buccaneers), one thing is certain: the team's brand is worth substantially more than it was in 1994.

How much more? $4.2 billion more. The Pats are now worth $4.4 billion, making them the second-most-valuable team in the NFL.

Bob Kraft probably isn't selling the team anytime soon, but the lesson stays the same. Whether you end up selling your life's work or not, doing the work in Branding For Buyout will make what you have more valuable.

Now, let's talk about the specific lessons you can take from this case study.

Traditional Exit Team (Siloed, Incomplete)

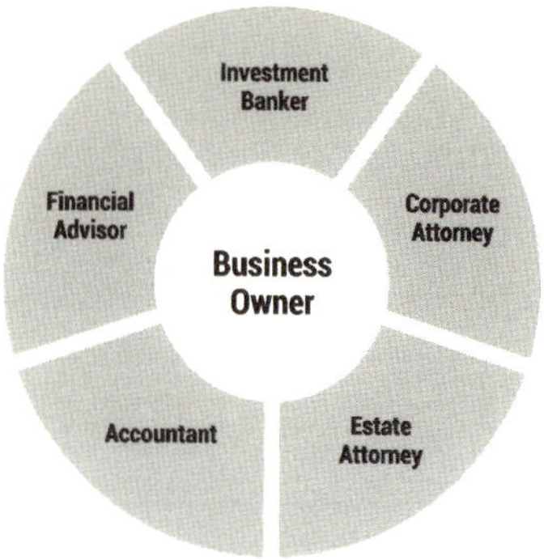

Nobody at this table (besides the owner) is solely responsible for revealing and creating value.

Optimized Exit Team (Integrated, Holistic)

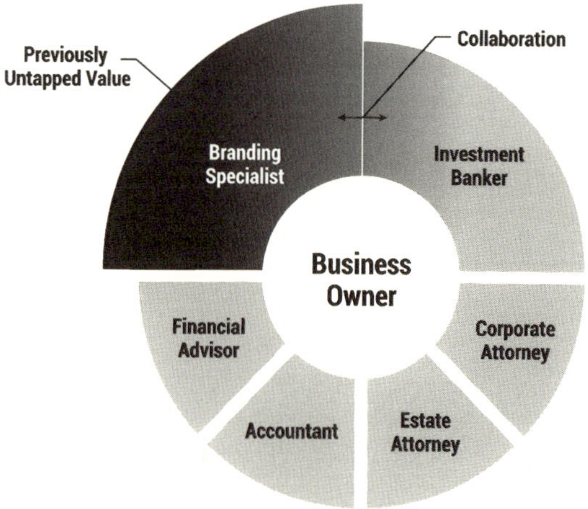

A dedicated Branding Specialist works in parallel with an Investment Banker to make the pie (potential sale price) larger.

Look for the human story.

Every single company in the United States has a set of financials, even if they're rudimentary. You need to know the numbers, and you need to see the trends, potential, and risks they represent. Think of that as the necessary part of your job as an entrepreneur, CEO, or owner, but don't stop there. What is the human story that goes with your financials? Why are you making the thing you're making? How did you discover it was something people needed? Why should somebody work with *you* instead of finding somebody else? A cynic might say that you don't need a human angle to sell B-to-B software, or do forensic accounting, or sign up more interstate truck leases than anybody else. But if you don't see the distinction between your idea and your company, your customers won't, either.

Before you decide to go find some stock images of athletic-looking people to put on your website, with some made-up quotes to provide this "human" touch, be careful. "Authenticity" is a word that gets thrown around a lot, especially now that some companies have caught on to the idea that telling a backstory is something that connects you to a customer. You've certainly seen plenty of beautifully staged photographs with folks describing the first axe they borrowed from their grandfather and why it inspired these particular $200 boots, or how this $65 bourbon is made with the same recipe brought over on the Mayflower in 1620. If those stories are true, that's great. But when you can tell the story and also show its authenticity, that's even better.

I'll give you an example. During my work with BrassRing, we designed a clever internal careers website with a then-new technology called Flash, which let users play a kind of interactive game as they learned about the company. You maneuvered your character through a maze of choices, and if you "won" the game, you earned the brass ring (get it?). It wasn't rocket science, but it was certainly a good 10 years before the trend you see now, where everything is gamified.

The BrassRing game was welcomed by younger potential employees—exactly for whom it was designed. It was also a powerful tool for BrassRing salespeople. They showed external clients how the company did things on its own internal site, so the client could relate to it: "Want to see what we're going to do for you? It's an extension of what we do for our own team."

BrassRing's Gary Cormier understood the value of that concept from the beginning, because he had lived it, all the way back to his days at Lotus. "When we came out with Lotus Notes, the email software, we knew immediately that the only way we would be able to sell it is if we were committed, enthusiastic users of it," he says. "That meant designing it in a thoughtful way ahead of time, and being able to show the market authentically how we eat our own dog food, so to speak. If we couldn't show what the practical applications were for our own products, what would be the point?"

Don't get lost in describing the features.

One of the most common conversations I have with new

clients about the whole brand story concept happens when I ask what makes their thing stand out. They almost always start with one of its features. It's bigger. Faster. The processor works better. It has fewer calories and no artificial ingredients. Those are great to have, and I'm not discounting them, but they aren't the core of your brand or your brand story. When you think about Porsche, you don't immediately say to yourself, yeah, that's the company that makes the sports car with the engine in the back and the leather seats that are super nice, and the SUV that has 500 horsepower and can raise and lower itself. You might remember one of its slogans: "Porsche. There is no substitute."

Now, having a rear-mounted, high-powered engine and other performance features does contribute to making a fast, desirable car—but the brand story is that Porsches are the best, and if you get something else, you're settling.

Ask for second opinions.

You're going to tell me that nobody knows your business like you do, and I won't argue with you. You're probably right, but that knowledge isn't enough. In fact, in many cases, that knowledge can hurt you. It prevents you from asking a potential client some questions about its big picture—what is the client's plan for your business? As you'll see in several of the case studies coming up, getting lost in the little things can actually obscure your view of the big-picture strategy.

Asking outsiders you trust to tell you what they see—and

actually listening to that feedback—are extremely powerful and valuable. You'll certainly hear some things you didn't want to hear, but that gives you the chance to address them and turn them into value producers, not value drains. It will be jarring at first to hear people poke holes in what is probably your life's passion, but if you can stand for it and take the value of the analysis, your business will be better for it.

It's also important to say out loud that none of us is good at everything! I know ninja-level creative people who miss every deadline and can't remember clients' first names. There are Olympic-level tech people who can build their own supercomputer but can't grasp basic accounting. Whether it's finance, sales, client relations, marketing, or any other facet of your business, getting other opinions about what works and what doesn't is extremely valuable. That's especially true in legacy businesses that have been doing things a certain way for a long time. Some processes are awesome because they're tried and true. Others are just rusty, like printing out an invoice and mailing or faxing it to a client when there's a cheap, time-saving, work-consolidating, digital solution.

BrassRing was as connected with its customers as any organization I've ever seen. They had a client board set up with some of their biggest accounts, and they'd meet four times a year to discuss trends and issues in the world of talent management, and how BrassRing could potentially build solutions to the client's problems. But it's very easy to get so engrossed in those problems that you lose some of the wider view. You don't see the forest for the trees. Bringing in the right outside set of eyes gave BrassRing some wider context for what they were doing, and it injected some new ideas to mix with what they were already doing well.

Don't be afraid to ask for second opinions about your business. You might even hear something that could move your business into a different—and far more profitable—space you had never imagined, with clients and partners (or acquirers) you had never considered.

CHAPTER 2

David vs. Goliath: Do You Know Your Market?

As a pre-revenue start-up in the newly conceived "hot cloud storage" space, Wasabi had an undeniably audacious goal: Take on Amazon...and win. Industry veterans David Friend and Michael Welts came to me through a friend's referral and got right to the point in our first meeting. "Want to help us build a brand? You have seven days to show us your ideas." The vacation I was about to start with my family turned into a trip where I spent most of my time in the hotel room, grinding on concepts with the team. But when I heard their vision—turning storage into a commodity, like electricity—I knew I wanted in. The mission was clear. Build a provocative, global challenger brand from scratch, challenge Amazon, and disrupt the market. What an opportunity, and I'm thrilled I got to go along for the ride.

David Friend's story as an entrepreneur is about as rock-and-roll as it gets in the world of tech.

At Yale in the late 1960s, he had an unlikely double major. Composing music was his passion, while engineering satisfied his family's desire for him to be able to get a "real" job. Friend's first job out of school was a bit of both. He helped start ARP Instruments, the first brand to make high-quality electronic synthesizers that were both good enough to do stage and studio duty for demanding professional musicians like The Who and Led Zeppelin, and cheap enough to be accessible to the average amateur garage band.

ARP became the dominant player in the space, relying on word-of-mouth marketing and endorsements from musicians of every genre. Stevie Wonder used one of ARP's "2600" models, with a customized control panel printed in Braille. An ARP synthesizer-keyboard made the famous five-note sequence used to communicate with the aliens in Steven Spielberg's *Close Encounters of the Third Kind.*

But as the 1970s came to a close, David could see where the instrument manufacturing business was headed. Even though he had spent a decade establishing ARP's footprint in music stores and on arena stages around the world, Japanese competitors were able to produce synthesizers with equal performance at a fraction of the price.

The experience was a jumping-off point that turned into a succession of entrepreneurial ventures, ranging from one of the earliest large-scale computer graphics companies to data-storage company Carbonite, which David Friend and Jeff

Flowers started in 2006. After Friend's daughter lost a college term paper to a crashed hard drive, and two years of baby pictures on Mrs. Flowers's computer met the same fate, Friend and Flowers built Carbonite to be an always-connected, online data backup service that would be cheap and "point-and-click" simple for everyday use. By 2011, they were backing up more than a billion files for one million customers, and they took the company public. After moving away from their everyday roles at Carbonite as CEO and CTO, Friend and Flowers were looking for their next foray into tech, and they found it in a line of business closely related to the one they just left, but with an important twist.

The concept for Wasabi—the company they founded in 2017—was born from a data-storage innovation Flowers came up with, improving on the technology that underpinned Carbonite. Customers could use the cloud not just as a warehouse for backup data, but as an extension of the working storage available on a desktop. Friend and Flowers avoided constructing a network with elaborate protocols that would make it hard for customers to migrate their data elsewhere. Now the partners would be competing with Amazon's formidable Amazon Web Services (AWS) platform. They developed cloud storage that would write fast and cheap with few barriers. The goal was to turn cloud storage into a commodity that customers would evaluate on price, speed, and reliability—like electricity—making it a business Amazon would most likely buy before it took the trouble to compete.

Friend knew that leaning heavily on just the technology

would make the brand susceptible to the same innovations that broke a company like Blockbuster Video and forged one like Netflix. Blockbuster did not foresee (or ignored) a market where customers didn't need to go to a store to get a physical copy of a movie they wanted to see. Netflix? You may not even remember that it used to be a company that mailed you DVDs, and waited for you to mail them back in when you were finished watching them.

"That's definitely a mistake I made back in the ARP days," David says. "We were in the dominant position then, and it was easy to look at all the endorsements from all these world-famous bands as proof we were doing what we should be doing. But we didn't see the risks until it was too late."

Friend recognized that the value of establishing the brand was just as important as the technology behind it. With the new Friend–Flowers venture, they would make sure to pre-engineer it before the first customer sale, to rope off its space in this new cloud-storage category.

A superficial look at the cloud-storage landscape in 2017 would make most people think Friend and Flowers were nuts for trying to play in that space. Amazon Web Services' client list was a murderers' row of powerful tech, entertainment, and government organizations—Netflix, LinkedIn, ESPN, the U.S. State Department. Google had its own impressive roster, with PayPal, Twitter, and UPS. Apple and Google already had storage options in their operating systems, for people who wanted to store more iTunes purchases or back up pictures from their smartphones. Microsoft, with its own storage options, leveraged its Outlook email platform as the gateway for corporate users' cloud-storage needs.

But for all of those big organizations' firepower, Friend also understood the way new lines of business were evaluated by companies like Amazon or Google. Below a certain financial threshold, these new businesses didn't even register. At the price and speed Friend knew he could deliver cloud-storage services to mid-size clients, the giants in the space probably wouldn't bother to compete—at least, not in the beginning. If Friend and Flowers could tell the right story, and deliver on what they promised, they'd have time to stake out that territory. "It sounds old-fashioned," says Friend, "but in the literal sense, it has always been about going out and putting boots on the ground—going to trade shows, asking customers questions, really examining what competitors and potential competitors were doing. And then it's about telling a story that means something."

The first challenge? Getting the name right.

In its incubation phase, Wasabi wasn't even Wasabi. Its placeholder name was Blue Archive—Friend's favorite color, along with a "civilian" term representing what the technology would be doing. Friend and Flowers knew they needed to bring in an experienced marketer to build the company's brand story from scratch, so they convinced Michael Welts to leave Google-backed start-up Plexxi to come in as chief marketing officer.

Welts explains, "The mission right from the start was to take on Amazon, Google, and Microsoft—which means we couldn't get any venture capital, because they all said, who

Cloud Storage Revenue—IDC Worldwide Semiannual Public Cloud Services Tracker, 2H19

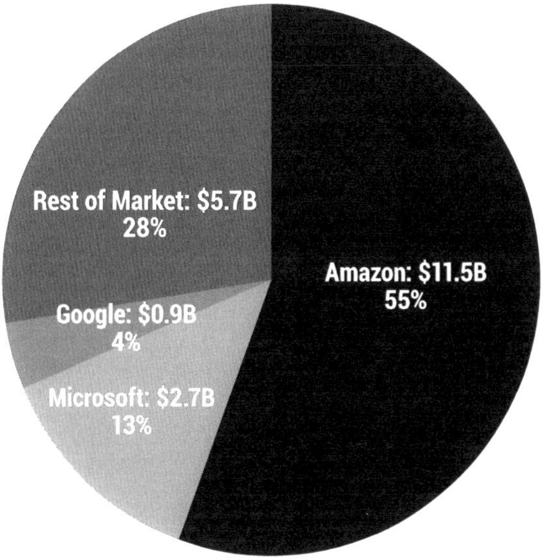

Amazon, Google, and Microsoft combined generated more than $15 billion in annual cloud storage sales in 2019—of which Amazon did 55 percent.

would take them on? But when David started Carbonite, nobody would take on IBM, EMC, and HP. Three years later, those companies were out of the business Carbonite was in."

In his first week at the company, Welts set up the same fact-finding process he had at other start-ups. He introduced Friend and Flowers to an experienced intellectual-property attorney, and instructed Flowers—the chief technology officer—to brief the attorney on why the company's technology would be sustainable and resistant to early obsolescence.

After Flowers described the concept of dirt-cheap, instant-access, cloud-based archiving, Welts's story gears started to turn. "What is the stuff on your desktop called? Active data. And what's another term for active data? Hot data," says Welts. "And that was it. We had a category, and we had a story. Hot cloud storage—storage where you won't even know the difference between storing it locally and on the cloud."

Everything about the company's "Blue Archive" placeholder name pointed to the past when it came to storage—cold, time-consuming, archival. On the other hand, the word "wasabi" had a completely different connotation. It was a word that worked across languages—like Amazon or Google—and immediately triggered something. If you've tasted wasabi, you remember the sensation. Vividly. "With that name, we had half of our new category coming out of people's mouths," recalls Welts. Amazon's competing product? The cold, distant-sounding Glacier—which took hours to retrieve your information (literally) from cold storage.

The strategy? Tell the David vs. Goliath story of a new, challenger brand ready to give you the service you need, faster and cheaper but just as securely as the big guys at Amazon, Google, and Microsoft. David and Michael set me to work with one of my favorite design briefs ever: Challenge Amazon.

We quickly mapped out the bones of a scalable campaign and brand look, voice, and feel. It started with the provocative "Welcome to the Jungle, Amazon" headline—which asked potential customers a very simple question. If all fast, reliable storage is pretty much the same, why pay more than you have to? Within three months, we had built Wasabi's entire communications infrastructure and gotten Wasabi's small, internal team fired up for guerrilla warfare.

Wasabi's goal was to pull in 100 corporate customers in the first year. Within eight months, Wasabi had more than 1,000, and 20,000 signed up within three years. Because of the legwork Friend and Flowers did ahead of time, they knew that Amazon, Google, and Microsoft would not initially clamor to gain share in a space where they were five times as expensive and half as fast. The first mover with the strongest brand awareness would have a massive advantage in this wide open space, and this advantage would also make it resistant to upstart challengers. "We built the brand for mindshare, not market share," says Welts. "A venture capital company will say, if Wasabi is already in control of this category, how much money are we going to have to pump into this brand to take it away from them? Or what have you come up with that's better than what they do? Which isn't possible yet. So, in a sense, the VCs are actually blocking for us right now."

But without delivering—without real-world believability—all the marketing in the world would only go so far. In a theme you will notice throughout this book, the entrepreneur took advantage of his size to behave in a way his larger competitor couldn't or wouldn't. Wasabi was small and adaptable, so it could offer a legitimate free trial for its enterprise storage solution: "Try it. See if it does what we say. Once we prove to you we can do it for that price and at that speed and reliability, your search will be over."

Amazon, Google, and Microsoft are giant providers with sprawling, bundled solutions that don't come *a la carte*. Using their storage requires a different kind of commitment across all of the computing, networking, and storage spaces. But there are plenty of companies that don't need (or can't afford!) a huge cross-platform solution for what to them is a relatively simple problem.

One of the reasons David Friend has been so successful at starting and building companies is because he's been able to see and understand the future—and position his companies where that future will be. With the help of "futurist" Tom Koulopoulos (with whom David wrote the influential book *The Bottomless Cloud* in 2019), we told the compelling story of what Wasabi would help everyone do. It wasn't just about providing for the huge storage needs of data-intensive organizations. It was about commoditizing storage, so anyone doing something requiring storage would essentially be turning on a light switch. When you turn on the light, there's abundant, cheap electricity available for as long as you need it. You don't even think about it anymore. That's where big data—the volumes of algorithmic raw material that drive everything from social media to advertising to insurance to traffic management—already operates. Think about the iPhone in your pocket. It takes super-high-resolution photos and creates files that would choke a phone from even five years ago. And that's just *your own* phone. Almost a billion people use iPhones every day. A Tesla electric car produces petabytes (a thousand trillion bytes!)

IDC Cloud Storage Standings

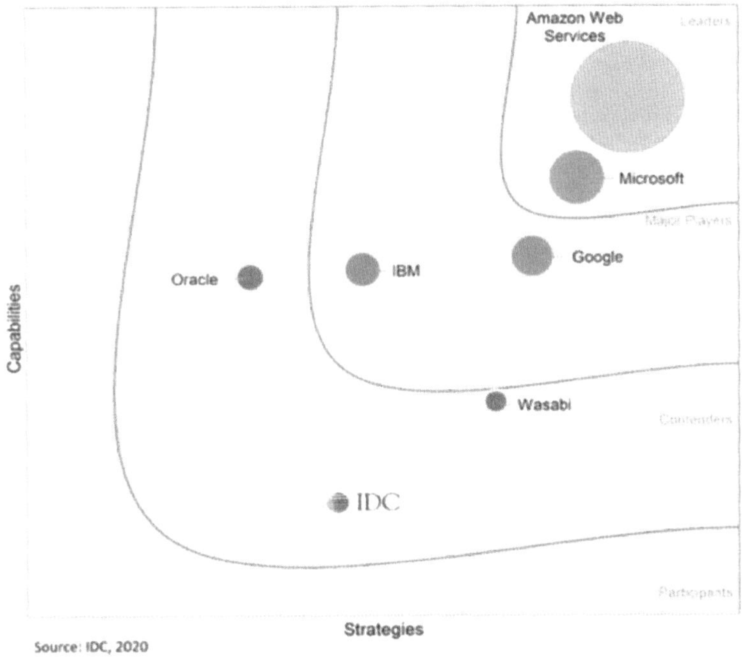

Of the companies competing in the cloud storage category, Wasabi is the only one solely focused on being a cloud storage vendor. Proving viability with analyst groups like IDC and Gartner can generate significant value in the market.

of data on every trip you take. Imagine the value of being the world's cheapest, most reliable vault for all that data.

It didn't take long for analysts to recognize Wasabi's market position. IDC is considered the international weather vane for market intelligence. Its research drives valuations, investment decisions, and Wall Street outlooks. When IDC identified

Wasabi as one of the contenders in the concentric ring just outside the dominant Amazon–Google–Microsoft trio (see graphic), it made Wasabi's market.

The challenges presented by COVID-19 only strengthened Wasabi's position. Companies like Legendary Entertainment, which made films in the *Jurassic Park* and *Batman* series, use Wasabi to allow creative teams operating remotely to do data-intensive work simultaneously, instead of transferring work piecemeal from station to station throughout the production process.

The technology behind Wasabi makes that kind of transformative shift possible, but the lesson for any entrepreneur isn't to go out and reinvent the wheel. Even if you do, explaining the physics of a cylinder vs. the physics of a cube is much tougher than saying how a cart with wheels is easier to move from the cave to the river. "In the tech space, product marketers tend to have an engineering background, and they immediately go into the features—the feeds and speeds," says Welts. "But when you talk to the C-level people at a company, they don't care about the infrastructure. They want to hear about how you're going to make them safe, reliable, productive, and most importantly, competitive."

Michael actually avoids learning too much about the technical guts inside the servers at Wasabi's data centers in Oregon, Virginia, Holland, and Japan. He wants to stay "free" enough to tell how Wasabi can solve specific problems for one of its potential partners—say, an information technology supplier that needs to temporarily access and move client data in real time. Does it matter how the data gets to Oregon? Or is it more important that the data is safe and instantly accessible, and the service is cheap enough that the client can bundle the service as a part of its fee and make a comfortable profit margin?

I realize that this concept might be at odds with your reality as the intimately involved, live-and-breathe-the-company entrepreneur. You just can't "forget" what you know about your business. But there is untapped value in embracing the spirit of the concept. If you took away the ability to talk about specific features and processes related to your brand, how would you tell your story to a potential customer? Taking that one step further, how would the competitors in your space do it? If a new competitor in your space could inspire genuine fear, what story would they tell?

That isn't some kind abstract thought exercise. Abraham Maslow's research on human psychology from the 1930s is imprinted in the DNA of virtually all modern marketing. Maslow's *Hierarchy of Needs* established the baseline requirements all humans have—physiological needs like air, food, and water—and examined how the needs of security, socialization, and self-actualization built on that framework. The *Harvard Business Review* worked in conjunction with Bain & Company to produce a modernized version of Maslow's hierarchy (shown on the next two pages), which is pretty much a primer on where the modern American consumer lives every day.

Which of these needs would potential competitors be trying to meet? You may discover from this exercise that your

What Do You Need?

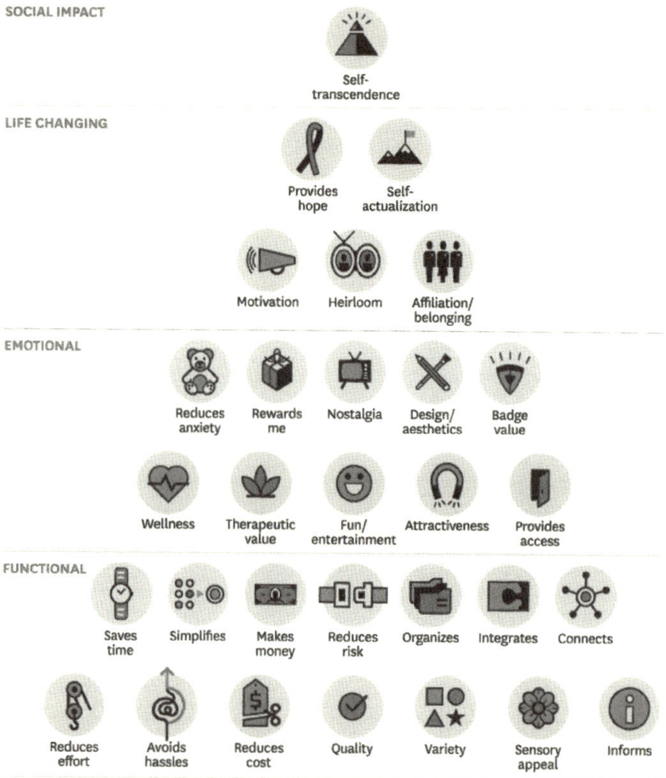

SOURCE © 2015 BAIN & COMPANY INC.
FROM "THE ELEMENTS OF VALUE," SEPTEMBER 2016

© HBR.ORG

The Elements of Value Pyramid

Products and services deliver fundamental elements of value that address four kinds of needs: functional, emotional, life changing, and social impact. In general, the more elements provided, the greater customers' loyalty and the higher the company's sustained revenue growth.

Psychologist Abraham Maslow devised this pyramid of human needs for a 1943 article in *Psychological Review,* and it's been a fundamental in branding and marketing since. The more of these needs a brand can meet—and the higher it can go on the pyramid—the more loyalty it can create. The chart on the next page shows the *why* behind the *what*. The lower bands on the chart are the basic costs of entry and competence. The bands at the top are where we focus our differentiation efforts.

Why Do You Need It?

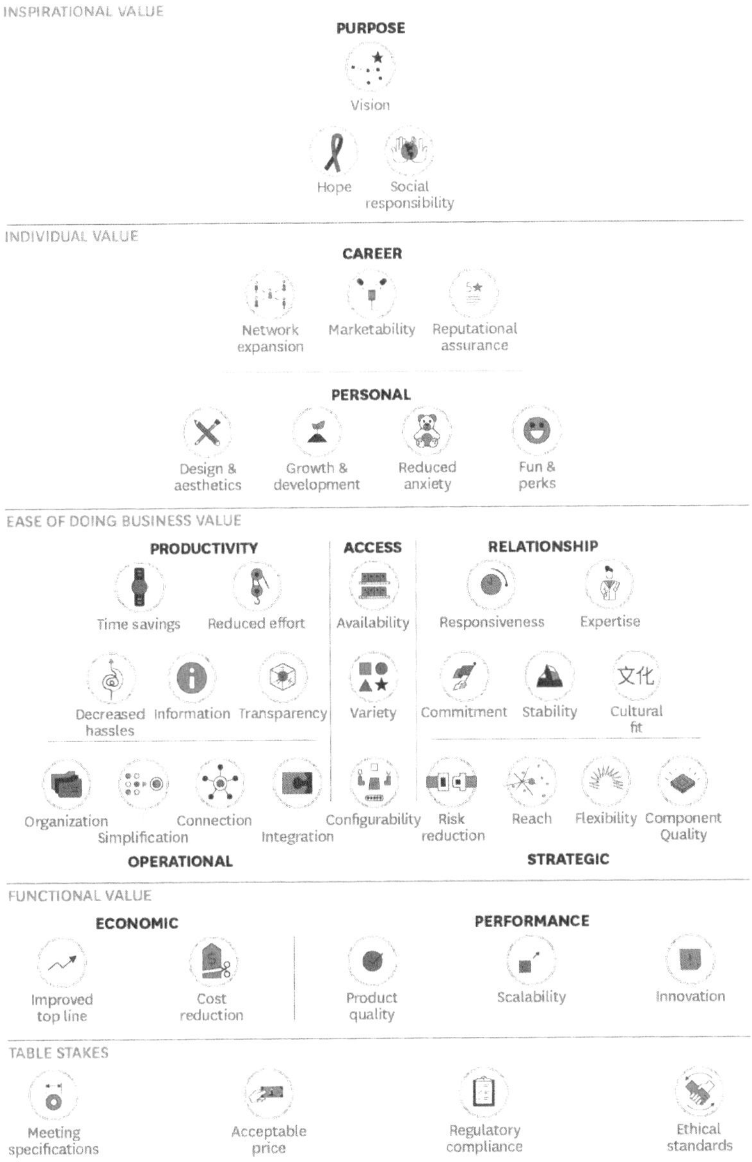

attention needs to be focused on players that haven't entered the space yet, and what you have to do to be ready when that happens.

Let's look at the other main lessons you can apply to your own situation.

Define your own category.

This is easier said than done, and easier in some categories than others, but the bigger overall point is that spending real time identifying the true category for your brand and your business—and targeting a category where you can be the leader or a legitimate challenger—has concrete benefits in its own right. More often than not, the process gives you leading indicators for potential market strategy. I'll give you an example.

In 2012, we started working with Sperry, the brand responsible for the Top-Sider (A/O Authentic Original) boat shoes every college kid was wearing at the time. Nobody is more aware of the potential booms and busts in the lifestyle space than the folks who are a part of that category. My friend Karen Pitts was the vice president of marketing for Sperry, and she knew that the "trendiness" part would fade to a degree, and the question was always going to be what was next. The difference was that she was asking those questions for the brand *while* Sperry was hot, so they could be ready for the next thing.

Boat shoes might have been what the trend-setting frat boys were wearing at Clemson, but they had originally been designed in the mid-1930s for a specific purpose—to maintain traction on slippery surfaces like a dock or a sailboat deck. One winter, Paul Sperry saw that his cocker spaniel, Prince, was able to make his way across ice without slipping when his human companion was simultaneously falling on his butt. Sperry examined Prince's paws and found the grooves that provided the necessary traction. He went home and carved similar "wave siping" into a piece of rubber sole, and the Top-Sider was born. The soles on the shoes have sipes similar to the ones on snow tires, which both push away water and add extra grip.

Where else would an innovative water/lifestyle brand story play? We saw that "action" water sports like stand-up paddleboarding were starting to pop, and the demographics for the people involved in those activities were super strong—avid participants who spend a lot of time and money. Better yet, those markets had size to them, relatively speaking, compared to the tiny subsets of people sailing and powerboating.

Our advice was to hit that market hard, and use the sales channels that were already in place at boating-specific retailers to expand the product line. At the biggest outdoor sports trade shows, Sperry was ready to go, reinforcing that the brand was much more than surfing a trend (so to speak). It was the dominant leader and the long-established brand in a hot, new, emerging space. That was an extremely powerful message to send, especially to the market in the rest of the world that wasn't too concerned with what college kids thought was cool at the moment.

We asked Sperry one main question: *If Nike owned the "Air," why couldn't Sperry own the water?* With the brand's

Sperry Brand Platform

ADVANCED WATER TECHNOLOGIES™

For the Advanced Water Technologies (AWT) platform, we created a logic behind Sperry product development and a storyline for consumers that focused on needs identification, technology, solutions, and performance benefits. By creating an association of "inspiration, technology, and experience," including a library of visual assets, we charted a new course for Sperry Top-Sider that helped the company research unique and specific solutions for serious athletes across paddle, boat/fish, and sail categories.

SPORT	INSPIRATION	TECHNOLOGY	EXPERIENCE
PADDLE	Paddlers face rocky trails, sandy streams, and blind seabeds. "When portaging, you're feeling your way through the water because you just can't see what's underneath."	SON-R Allows you to respond to what's underfoot.	See With Your Feet™
BOAT/FISH	Boaters and anglers face waves, engine vibration, and g-forces. "You have to protect your hips and joints from the pounding to make it through the day."	ASV Disperses shock and vibration forces.	Stop Shock & Vibration™
SAIL	Sailors face shifting winds, big waves, and tricky conditions. "You have to have really good grip. If your feet move at all, game over, you're out of the boat."	GRIP 3 Provides ultimate 360-degree grip.	Grab More Grip™

A version of "platforming."

credibility and longevity, matched with the "Advanced Water Technologies" story we created, Sperry was able to talk about both the roots and the future in the same messaging. The company could reclaim its performance heritage.

It's hard to put a precise value on what that meant for the value of the Sperry brand, because it was part of Collective Brands Performance + Lifestyle Group, which was owned by Payless—a group that also included Keds, Saucony, and Stride Rite. However, Sperry was the fastest-growing brand in that portfolio, and two months after we finished our three-year-plus run with Sperry, Wolverine Worldwide bought the entire brand portfolio for $1.2 billion.

Outliers are great. As long as there's a market.

In marketing we joke all the time about unicorns—brands that do the impossible and check off every single box for potential market, positioning, expertise, leadership, and financing. Right now, Amazon is a unicorn. I'm not doing you much of a service if the sum of my advice is "be like Amazon."

Unicorns are unicorns because they're rare!

Still, there's a lesson to be learned—and it might not be the one you think. As I said in the last section, the goal is to identify a category where you can be the winner or one of the top challengers. Did Amazon set out with the ultimate goal to be the leader in online book sales? No, that was a waypoint toward its completely audacious, master-of-the-universe goal, which was to practice with training wheels on a predictable market (books) and use that experience to eventually sell everything to everybody. The advantages Amazon had (and has) are time and money.

As you review some of the steps and processes I talk about in this book, and you study and sculpt and excavate your way to a breakthrough on what your category and brand vision should really be, you should pause. Think about what the final analysis might look like.

Is the market ready for what you have to offer? Is there a mechanism in place to deliver it?

Think hard about those questions, because the wrong answers can be painful.

Years ago, before Wasabi, Michael Welts was the CEO of a start-up that perfected a kiosk-based interface for quick-service restaurants that cut order time from a minute and half to 11 seconds. He got a commitment from Bain Capital to come in with venture cash, and Dunkin' was investigating using it across its hundreds of locations in the northeast. But Bain came to the conclusion that the market wasn't ready for mass adoption of machines in the place of a human taking an order, and declined to fund. Michael had to sell off the intellectual property as spare parts.

In both of these examples, would these be categories where you could establish leadership? Absolutely. Impossible Burgers proved it in the grocery space. They convinced grocers to stock their plant-based "meat" right alongside real ground beef in the refrigerator case, which made the consumer's shopping easier. And kiosks? After we'd all spent a few years getting accustomed to using them to check into flights at the airport, McDonald's bought into them, too—and they're rolling them out across the country, just as the world has become way more interested in "touchless" experiences, thanks to the COVID-19 pandemic.

You need to be right, at the right time.

Play to your size.

Most people think a huge company like Amazon has virtually unlimited advantages. It can spend whatever it wants, hire (almost) whoever it wants, and make the markets it wants to enter. All of those things are true, but what David Friend demonstrated so clearly with Wasabi is that there are plenty of things big players don't and *can't* do.

It is inherently difficult for a large company to move quickly and change direction. Small start-ups can find and thrive in niches that aren't worth the big companies' efforts. Start-ups are in a better position to see granular local or regional trends and actually act on them.

The more you build systems that mimic a larger company's, the more you give that movement advantage back to the larger competitor. It's something to be particularly cautious about if you leave a large organization to do your own entrepreneurial thing. Deb Besemer from BrassRing (discussed in the last chapter) worked from companies ranging in size from start-up to giant. "When you work for a large company and go to a small company," says Besemer, "the skill you need is the ability to recognize what your company will need as it gets bigger, but build it incrementally so you don't burden your small company with policies and procedures. Do you need a suite of complicated software for billing and CRM, or can you do that with a spreadsheet until you're bigger? Those decisions permeate everything you do in a small company. The mistake a lot of entrepreneurs make is putting too many 'big company' things in place too soon. You lose the advantage of speed."

CHAPTER 3

Get Outside the Fishbowl: What Do You See?

Building Etonic was a three-year endeavor with lots of grinding and clawing from the day we started through the company's sale. From an initial catalog-design project, to a website, to a fully integrated partnership, we worked side by side with this team to do what seemed like the impossible: bring credibility back to a brand that was on the brink of oblivion. The result was the sale of an American-icon, multi-sport brand to a passionate Italian sportswear company for a healthy multiple.

For those too young to remember, Etonic was a *thing,* however briefly.

The shoe brand had more than a century of heritage that included outfitting the U.S. Army in combat boots during World War I, and outfitting some of the most famous golfers in the world in the 1950s and 1960s, but it was running and basketball that turned it into a legitimate competitor with Nike, Converse, and Adidas in the 1980s.

A year before Nike released its first Air Jordans, Etonic launched its Hakeem Olajuwon signature shoe in 1984, and the seven-foot-tall center quickly became one of the dominant players in the NBA. In running, the most famous marathoner in American history, Bill Rodgers, was Etonic's brand ambassador, and the four-time winner of both the Boston and New York marathons. For a long time, the two leading golf-shoe brands were FootJoy and Etonic.

But almost as quickly as it hit, it was over.

Parent company Colgate-Palmolive was struggling in 1985, so it looked to sell off brands that weren't tied to its core business, which made a shoe company an easy target. It sold Etonic to Artimas, the Swedish owners of the Tretorn shoe brand. Artimas brought in an experienced management team to turn it around, which returned the brand to prosperity. Etonic would end up being sold again in 1996, to global investment company KKR. The private-equity group was hoping to link Etonic's well regarded golf-shoe business with its Spalding and Top-Flite lines of golf equipment and compete with Titleist in the premium golf space. But by the early 2000s, Spalding was nearing bankruptcy and Etonic was a zombie brand, meaning just like it sounds: going through the motions, a dead brand walking. Spalding released a few moderately successful models of Etonic golf shoes, but stopped bothering to produce any other lines of Etonic shoes at all. They licensed the Etonic name for the running- and walking-shoe business lines to a small footwear producer, and the licensee pushed the Etonic shoes into as many retail outlets, including discount outlets, as it could.

By 2003, pieces of Spalding were being sold to generate cash, and the concept of rehabilitating Etonic as a stand-alone business piqued the interest of Dan Ladd and Karen Pitts, who had been the heads of sales and marketing at Dexter Golf. They took their idea to their former boss at Dexter, Ted Alfond. Ted didn't do deals, but he knew somebody who did—his son-in-law, Tom Seeman, who had just moved to Boston from Berlin, Germany.

Seeman convinced Spalding to split Etonic off from the rest of the golf division, and sell it to him for just over $5 million—which seems like a bargain until you consider that it was losing more than $2 million a year at the time, according to Seeman. The purchase price was all equity, because no bank was willing to be a part of the deal for the struggling brand.

Seeman saw three attributes in Etonic buried under layers of dust and neglect. The brand had an amazing, 140-year-old backstory in American shoemaking. It still retained a strong reputation in markets outside the United States, but it wasn't getting enough value from any product line outside of golf shoes. Seeman also had talented and enthusiastic young industry veterans in Ladd and Pitts to help him with the renovation—starting with conceiving and designing an exciting new golf shoe, which was the core of Etonic's sports history.

"The first job was to get back the license, so we could stop the damage to the brand and realize the dream of being a multi-sport brand again," says Seeman. "We were able to show that, per the terms of the licensing agreement, our shoes weren't supposed to be in places like Costco—and that even though the licensee was making something they called "walking shoes," which they said fell under their license to produce athletic shoes, what they were making were basically brown leather shoes with Etonic logos on them."

After successfully terminating the license, Seeman began to ramp up Etonic's presence in a few niche markets to re-establish its credibility. He needed to rebuild trust with both potential customers and within the industry, most of which had written Etonic off as a zombie brand. Some of that trust was built in, because Seeman had Ladd and Pitts on the team. "Bowling is a small, niche business, but it's profitable, and the management team had a lot of expertise in it," says Seeman. "We launched a bowling line, and that made us some money, so we were eventually profitable in golf and bowling. That meant it might be time to get back into running and walking."

It's not an accident that your Instagram and Facebook feeds are filled today with all kinds of brand stories highlighting things like "heritage" and "legacy" and "tradition." There's more trust available for a company that has been around for decades, and having an extended past offers so much more raw material to form the basis of a compelling story. The brand might be new, but the origin story links it to the building the company occupies, the profession of the founders' ancestors, or the heritage of the city where the brand is located.

Of course, when that heritage doesn't exist, marketers try to find some. Lifestyle brand Shinola took its name from the old shoe-polish brand. Detroit is a fundamental part of Shinola's product lineup and marketing, and the company has invested millions in repurposing General Motors' old research facility into its headquarters and production space, and training Detroiters to make watches. Still, Shinola was founded by a brand management company in Texas that saw an opportunity to capitalize on Detroit's underdog status and manufacturing tradition, and used it to sell $600 watches.

Shinola made up its own story, but Etonic had a genuine story to mine, from being a World War I boot supplier to producing the first golf-specific shoe in 1945 and innovating in the lightweight-running-shoe category in the 1970s and '80s. The roots of the company went back to the late 1800s, when Brockton, Massachusetts, was the shoe capital of the United States—with factories employing more than 30,000 workers. The Charles Eaton Company—Etonic's ancestor—was one of the first and among the biggest. "The revival of authentic brands is something the trade press always likes to talk about," observes Tom Seeman, "and we got a lot of attention for buying the brand and announcing that we wanted to build on old technologies and get back into running shoes."

In an ironic bit of providence, shoe innovator Martin Keen had been pushed to the side at KEEN, the sandal company he co-founded, when new investors came in. So he was available to join Etonic as a consultant and immediately inject expertise and credibility into the new ownership's first running-shoe line, which debuted in 2006. "I didn't know footwear, and I didn't know how to design and make a shoe in China," says Seeman. "But I had a great team around me, and I knew from them and from learning all about the business during my first three years we were in it that to get real, sustained credibility as a technical running brand—to get placement in the technical running shops and the attention of the serious runners—and to be able to use that success to eventually move into larger stores with higher volumes of less technical footwear, that was going to take a lot of investment."

So Seeman and Etonic reached a crossroads that needs to be as recognizable for a start-up entrepreneur as it was for a veteran of several exits. Would Etonic's ownership group invest more capital into the brand to push the expansion farther, faster? Would it sell off a chunk of the brand to a new investor? Or was it time to position Etonic for a sale and full exit?

The notion of getting out so soon—relatively speaking—was natural for Seeman. "Everything in the financial analysis pointed that this was the right move," he says. "We had gone from losing more than two million a year to being profitable. Our sales were up every year. It was the perfect story to help sell the company. There were no breaks in those rising sales-and-profits lines from year to year. I knew that if we decided to go into technical running big-time, all of those smooth sales-and-profits lines would be broken up. Maybe we'd finally get there, but then it would have to be on just the beautiful storyline, or a revived brand could possibly be lost if we failed in the running category. Running would be a big risk for us, and I felt we had already taken enough risk—I thought we should let the next owner invest in running. I thought we'd get a phenomenal return on our invested money if we sold the company now."

Seeman and his team got to work.

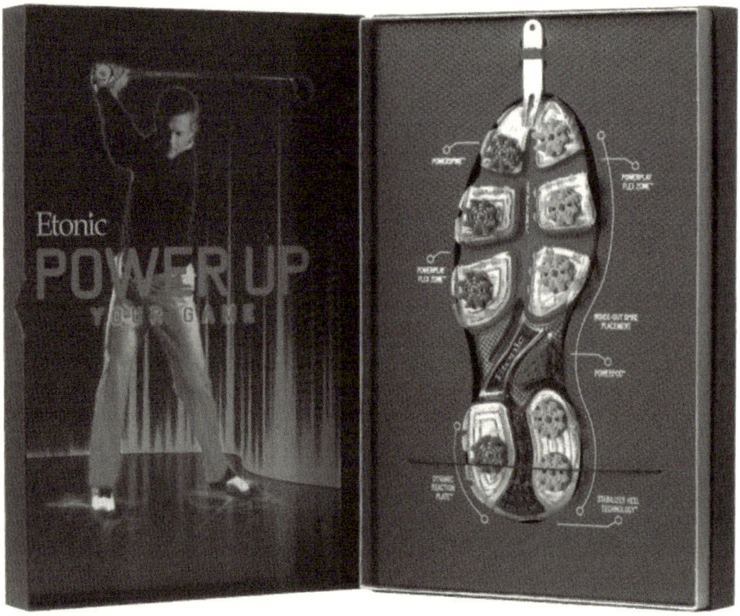

Direct marketing "clutter buster" sent to golf pro shops to highlight the new Etonic outsole innovation.

The first task was to firmly establish Etonic as both a brand with multiple product lines and one with an innovative future. The collaboration with Martin Keen was part of that on the product, but it also meant bringing in my team to help Karen Pitts drive Etonic's marketing message worldwide. How did you do that in the early days of web marketing, in a field that was dominated by big players like Nike, Adidas, and FootJoy?

We sharpened Etonic's legacy story by mixing it with the story of one of golf's hot young players, who could also provide the "local boy makes good" angle—Boston's James Driscoll. Etonic had been trusted by PGA Tour players for more than 50 years, and James was the latest in this long line—but his shoes were different than the ones your father would have worn. They were light, and lined with Gore-Tex so they were truly waterproof, not just "water resistant"—which was industry code for "soggy and heavy by the 14th hole." And Etonic was one of the first brands to sell golf shoes directly to the customer. The shoes now had plastic spikes in place of the traditional steel ones. The softer cleats were easier on the grass, and made the shoes more comfortable when walking on hard surfaces.

Etonic not only had an amazing, century-long heritage in the shoe business. It was also the trailblazer in a lot of ways we take for granted when it comes to shoes. The first company to make a dedicated golf shoe? Etonic. The first one to integrate waterproof Gore-Tex into golf shoes? The first to offer non-metal spikes standard? The first to base its golf-shoe sole on biomechanical stability research? Always Etonic. Those facts became the centerpiece of the creative we built, first for Etonic's catalog and then for its web presence and all of its advertising collateral: "First one there." Etonic was the brand where you could have the trust that came with being around for a century, plus the commitment to innovations that truly improved the golfer's competitive experience.

It was an exhilarating time, because Etonic was matching up against giants like Nike and FootJoy—which had virtually unlimited budgets—and was doing it on a literal shoestring. Karen Pitts had to scratch and claw for every dollar of marketing spend, and justify it by showcasing the response the brand was getting beyond sales figures. "I knew the history of the brand, and its history of innovation," says Pitts. "That great story was there to be told, and I knew the proof was there in the quality of the thinking behind the work we were doing. We were able to say we were more innovative than FootJoy and more credible than Nike—Nike was huge but had just recently dropped into the golf space."

Nike had the most famous athlete in the world, Tiger Woods, wearing its full line. Adidas bought the third-largest golf equipment manufacturer in the world, TaylorMade, and was integrating athletes using that gear into its shoe lines. It was a natural move to look at other golf-related brands with the budget to take on the biggest players, for a potential fit as an acquirer. Puma had entered the golf-shoe space, and Etonic would have worked well as a more traditional "performance" line to go with Puma's trendier, fashion-driven shoes.

Outside of golf, you could make the same kind of case. In the running-shoe business, New Balance was a strong performer in the high-end technical category. Etonic had even brought in former New Balance exec Gary Siriano to develop its running line, so there was a potential fit there. Etonic could have found a slot as a value category just below the New Balance line in price and features.

From another strategic perspective, Dick's Sporting Goods made sense as a buyer, too. The sporting-goods giant had been so important to Etonic's golf-shoe line because it had persistently carried the "little guy's" shoes to counterbalance massive displays from brands like Nike and FootJoy. Dick's had already purchased well-known brands like Slazenger clubs and Walter Hagen apparel, making those their in-house lines, and it would have made sense to get into the footwear space, too.

My job was to really emphasize the American tradition and international allure of the brand, and it paid off in the form of a buyer coming from a market Etonic hadn't expected. Lotto Sport Italia was (and is) a huge player in the European apparel and footwear space, selling everything from soccer cleats to track shoes to lifestyle clothing. It sponsors dozens of top teams in European soccer, and tennis legends like Martina Navratilova and Boris Becker wore Lotto when they were at their competitive peak.

What Lotto didn't have was much of a footprint in the United States. They had tried and failed to buy Brooks when it came up for sale in 2004, and were hungry to get into the market. Karen Pitts remembers, "We were a small company, and we needed to be careful about how we spent money, but I think one of our strengths was knowing how important the marketing would be to finding the right fit." Tom Seeman adds, "I can remember reading the first draft of the sales document from the investment bank we hired to help us sell Etonic, and it was very generic—'Etonic is a footwear brand with sales of such and such'—and I knew right away that wasn't going to matter as much as us showing we were about both heritage and innovation. The numbers were just a fraction of the story."

We framed what Etonic had—a long American tradition, a market share in sports where Lotto was nonexistent, and positive sales trends—not what it didn't have. This led Lotto chairman Andrea Tomat to see what Etonic could be when it was plugged into his ecosystem. The right kind of marketing and brand positioning made that possible. Lotto wasn't buying a zombie. It was buying something alive and growing. "Thanks to the great branding work, Etonic not only looked modern and relevant, but projected itself to be much bigger than the specific sales numbers indicated," says Pitts, who is now the general manager of specialty brands at Rockport. "The challenge has always been the same. How do you scale a brand? How do you bring it to life, articulate the 'why' first and run with it?"

Lotto was a strategic buyer, even if the market had a different frame than Tom Seeman and Etonic were considering at the time. But Andrea Tomat was also an emotional buyer. He had felt the pain of losing out whenever he tried to acquire a brand he wanted, and he was determined not to let the next one get away. That has to be a familiar feeling for anyone who has lost out on a house in a hot market. Potential transactions have become even more driven by analytics since this deal closed in 2006, but emotion and gut feelings are still factors. The goal of any brand and any marketer has to be to provide the story that can be an adaptable framework for the emotions and risks and excitement.

Tom Seeman, Karen Pitts, and Dan Ladd were generous enough to keep my team in place through the transition to Lotto ownership, which meant that we went to Italy to learn about the plans Lotto had for the new brand. It was fascinating—and rewarding—to see how Etonic would fit in with Lotto's bigger picture. Over a long dinner, some excellent wine, and a few cigars, Andrea would admit something you don't hear very many executives hot off an acquisition say. "We thought we bought something big and powerful, but the reality? Not so strong!" What should have been a proud moment really has an asterisk, and it's an asterisk we're going to talk about in a lot more detail in Chapter 6.

One of the (justifiable) raps marketing gets is that it's air. It's inventing something where nothing really exists. We showed Etonic in the best possible light, but it was Andrea's job to keep Etonic profitable after he bought it. There was also the concern that Lotto would be so enamored with making a line of fashionable running shoes that it would underestimate the importance of the golf line. (This would prove to come true later.) The fundamental principle of Branding For Buyout is that our mission is to reveal real value—not to sell a pig and find the right shade of lipstick to put on it.

Why?

Because real value is what consistently produces the

multiples—the exponential sale prices that separate fire-sale, pennies-on-the-dollar deals from ones that pay out in a big way, justifying the thousands of hours of time, effort, and sweat an entrepreneur has put in.

Anybody can win the lottery once. But planning to win the lottery isn't a sustainable business. That's why we're talking about real, concrete strategies, not short-term tricks.

Let's look at three of the main takeaways from this case.

Clean up the house.

Positioning the brand so that a potential acquirer can see how it could grow is obviously a key element in maximizing value. But one process that often gets overlooked is doing the intensive vetting of your entanglements—licensing arrangements, supplier agreements, intellectual-property contracts, non-compete agreements—to make sure you don't have any issues that could actually be a drain on your company's value.

Those kinds of entanglements are all examples of "paperwork" that can make it more difficult for an acquirer to get what it expects out of a purchase. In Tom Seeman's case, he was able to negotiate a competitive price when his group bought Etonic from Spalding, to spare the seller the potential hassle of dealing with the current athletic-shoe licensee. On the other side of the books, Seeman bought the brand as Spalding was about to enter bankruptcy, which caused that company's bankruptcy trustee to come looking for more cash from Etonic a year after the sale. By negotiating a deal that provided a cash stream to the trustee to satisfy other creditors, in exchange for managing some inventory and holding over some Spalding employees, Etonic was able to avoid getting tied up in long-term litigation that could potentially give an acquirer headaches.

By the time Seeman was ready to show Etonic to Lotto and other prospective buyers, the product lines were streamlined and organized, the point-of-sale visuals were new and fresh, and the website reinforced both the heritage of the past and the excitement in Etonic's future across all of golf, bowling, running, and walking.

Build credibility first, and volume later.

Scale is a word you'll hear five minutes into any conversation with venture capital, and for good reason. The scalability of a business directly affects its valuation. If what you're doing requires you to shake every hand personally, eventually you're going to run out of time in the day. But many, many brands focus strictly on scale, and forget the important steps that need to go first, as Karen Pitts said earlier.

Etonic's licensee didn't have any trouble with scale in terms of units sold. It unloaded inventory into outlet malls and discount stores. That practice could have continued indefinitely. But turning Etonic into an interchangeable commodity would have been a tremendous waste of all the equity and reputation built up over a century. The answer wasn't to sell more shoes immediately. It was to rebuild credibility in the right channels, where the brand could tell the full story of its innovation and leadership.

In Etonic's case, it meant demonstrating the heritage-plus-innovation story to the buyers inside the golf ecosystem first—the ones who decided what made it to the shelves in the high-end golf-apparel retail stores and country club pro shops. The Etonic brand already had historical traction with that group, so connecting the heritage to truly useful and unique innovations—like a lightweight, waterproof spikeless shoe constructed with attention to quality and detail—made the decision to both stock the shoe and promote it to customers much easier.

One example of this kind of promotion was retooling Etonic's tradeshow presence. The golf world convenes at the annual PGA Merchandise Show every January in Orlando, Florida, and thousands of buyers for clubs and shops around the world wander the floor of the convention center getting familiar with new products and submitting orders for the upcoming season. Big companies like Nike and FootJoy traditionally built elaborate booths that both showcased the new lines and gave reps comfortable places to do deals. Etonic's presence had dwindled under Spalding to the point that it was an afterthought—seen in a drab group booth.

One of our jobs was to remake the show experience (on a strict budget) in a way that would announce Etonic's new energy. We came up with a convertible space that could shift its shape to fit both the sprawling Orlando Convention Center floor and the smaller regional show spaces, and still show off the bold graphics and oversize photos of Etonic's exciting young brand ambassadors. The message? These aren't the Etonics your grandfather wore, but there's a reason they're still around.

Appeal to multiple markets.

One of the first pieces of research my team does when we get together with a new client is an immersive analysis of both the customer-side market for the brand and the landscape for potential acquirers. Two things are absolute facts. First, most entrepreneurs and owners have a good sense for which potential buyers are out there within their closest circle of competitors and strategic partners. After all, they're immersed in the market every day. Second, there are always, always potential buyers out there who would come as a complete surprise. Those can range anywhere from a financial buyer like a private-equity firm, to a buyer that just wants to close down the brand and protect its own market.

Many entrepreneurs, from the first moment they were in business, have operated with a specific buyer in mind—like Wasabi did with Amazon and Google. But whatever the size of the pool you're operating in, being able to identify potential buyers in multiple categories will expand the potential number of bids that ultimately come in. This is especially true when it comes to international markets. Most U.S. entrepreneurs think of domestic buyers as a matter of course, but Tom's previous international experience had broadened his horizons from the beginning of his time with Etonic, so a potential sale to a

European company was always a part of his thinking.

When Etonic went up for sale, 15 potential buyers went through the certification process to get access "under the hood" and see financials and other proprietary information. Footwear companies were obviously represented in that group, but there were also sporting-goods chains, private-equity groups, and individual regional buyers interested in the brand, for a variety of reasons and with a variety of potential strategies.

Framing the brand in a way that lets an acquirer see his or her future in it is a lot like staging a house in a neutral and attractive way when you put it up for sale. If the house is bare and empty, it can convey a kind of fire-sale desperation (and sadness!). However, if the house looks good and shows potential for expansion and new approaches, it will almost certainly invite buyers to look into it and imagine its possibilities.

Buyers Beyond Your Backyard

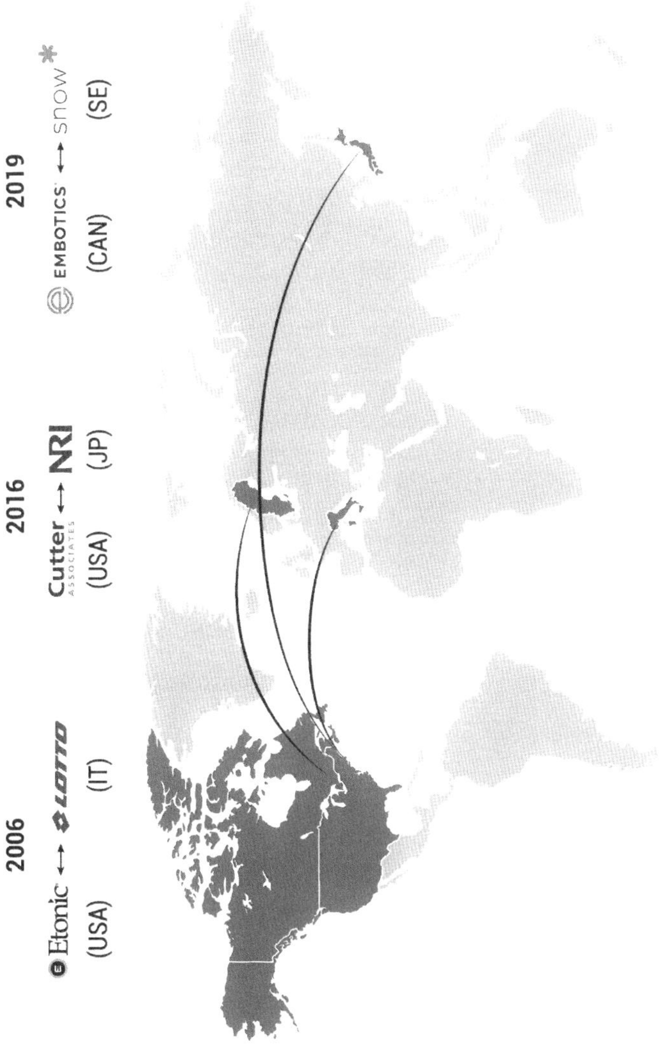

The markets around you are the easiest to see and study—but don't fall into the trap of failing to look outside those narrow borders. Many acquisitions happen when international firms are trying to gain a foothold in the U.S. market or export processes to less mature markets.

CHAPTER 4

When Lightning Strikes: Who Is on the Team?

What happens when a federal regulation is enacted that forces people to buy your product overnight? You strap yourself to a rocket and get ready for a wild ride. In this case the Environmental Protection Agency (EPA) did in fact pass a regulation that said if your house was built before 1978, you had to test for lead paint. Boom! LeadCheck grew 10x almost overnight. And to keep pace, its antiquated brand needed to be re-engineered almost as quickly as the business. This story is an exercise in the need for speed and an alert for acquisition by big business.

Want to know what a lightning strike looks like?

One of my favorite parts of this work is when a client and some really challenging-but-exciting market forces come together to produce an amazing opportunity—but only if we can execute a sophisticated brand-building campaign within a limited time.

That's where Hybrivet Systems was in 2010. An amazing confluence of events—a new government regulation and a window of time where this tiny company in Natick, Massachusetts, would have the only product of its kind in a huge, lucrative market—gave Hybrivet Systems an opportunity to set its brand up to be acquired for retire-early money.

But first, it would have to survive long enough to get to the exit.

Veteran sales and marketing executive Joe Moriarty took a drive over to Hybrivet's outdated, tiny office as a favor to a friend who knew the company was facing a once-in-a-lifetime opportunity—but one that required a different set of skills. Hybrivet's main brand, LeadCheck, had been doing steady if unspectacular business for 20 years. Invented by a former DuPont scientist, LeadCheck was a set of two chemicals that, when combined on a test strip, could reveal if the paint on a homeowner's wall or radiator contained lead.

Up until 2010, the market consisted mainly of parents who wanted peace of mind that their kids wouldn't get sick from ingesting lead paint. Then the EPA announced that any contractor who did work on a home built before 1978 would have to test the paint in the home for lead.

Twenty years earlier, LeadCheck founder Dr. Marcia Stone had patented the test, and eight years earlier, she went through the process to get the test recognized by the EPA. At the time of the EPA's announcement, LeadCheck was the *only* test on the market that a contractor could use to fulfill the requirement.

"On the first day I visited the office, I couldn't believe what I walked into," says Moriarty. "To say it was outdated would be an understatement. The office was straight out of the 1970s. They made the product by hand, using a nice group of about six employees."

Moriarty ran through LeadCheck's playbook with Dr. Stone. Was there any distribution to stores like Lowe's or Home Depot? None. All sales went through LeadCheck's antiquated website, and sales were fulfilled piecemeal out of the back of Hybrivet's office space.

Any forecast for what this would do to demand? Some were saying it could be a blip, Stone said.

Any way to ramp up production? No. Not without big investments in raw materials from chemical suppliers.

Moriarty signed on as LeadCheck's executive vice president of sales and marketing to take on the challenge. He recalls, "Three days later, when I came back on the day the rule was in place, the phone never stopped ringing from 6 a.m. to 10 p.m. Contractors, everyone. The buyer from Lowe's called and said they wanted to purchase 100 percent of manufacturing capacity for the next six months. We couldn't even do that, because of the orders we had already committed to through the website and what we had to supply to the EPA so they could do training."

The LeadCheck packaging hadn't been changed since it launched 20 years before. The package was an outdated clamshell that looked like a cigarette box, and none of it was designed to fit in a modern retailer's supply chain. The toughest part was that Dr. Stone's exclusive patent would expire in less than a year. Potential competitors would need time to wrestle with the EPA to get their competing products recognized, so LeadCheck had about 18 months to either strengthen the brand enough to survive an onslaught from giants like 3M, or make itself attractive enough to be bought by one of them.

"We had to start over," says Moriarty. "Branding, packaging, the boxes we would need to ship to retailers, everything."

And that's when I met Joe. Lightning had struck and Joe, instead of looking for somebody to put out the fire, needed help throwing more fuel on to get it burning hotter. As Joe called it, it was a problem-slash-opportunity.

Joe and his team were so busy just answering phones and taking orders that he needed some outside help to figure out exactly where LeadCheck stood, and where the potential threats—and opportunities—would be coming from.

Joe and I did a 360-degree brand review, and laid out all of the potential competitors. Three other companies had test kits that were in some phase of EPA evaluation—which would take at least a year. The competitors didn't have as elegant of a solution as LeadCheck's, which was simple interaction between two chemicals that produced a brilliant red mark on a test strip if lead was present. But they were all substantially better capitalized.

In our first few strategic conversations, we wanted to solve the branding and packaging problems. The potential for a sale was also in our peripheral vision, so we made some very specific bets on the brand where it would produce the most potential value. Walmart and Home Depot had requirements about what warning language needed to be on a retail package, and they also required that packaging have Spanish translations. So we knew that a comprehensive brand and packaging redesign that incorporated all of those elements in a coherent, intentional way made sense, as opposed to duplicating the effort later.

One inspiration was Apple, and what Steve Jobs was able to do with what anyone would consider a complicated device. For example, instead of a huge instruction manual with your iPhone, you get simple, beautifully packaged pieces that essentially tell you themselves how you're supposed to use them. There's no extra paper, clumsily wrapped headphones, or marketing material that looks out of place.

We radically streamlined LeadCheck's look, and made it a point to emphasize two basic elements. The first was fear. You, as a parent, don't want to risk your children's health, so you need to be safe. The second was trust and compliance. We're the only EPA-certified test, and you, as a contractor, can trust us to keep you from getting fined.

LeadCheck was easy to use and understand, it was reliable, and it tested down to the nanogram. We emblazoned a new tagline on the packaging that essentially told you everything you needed to know when you looked at your test results: "Red

Packaging: Before

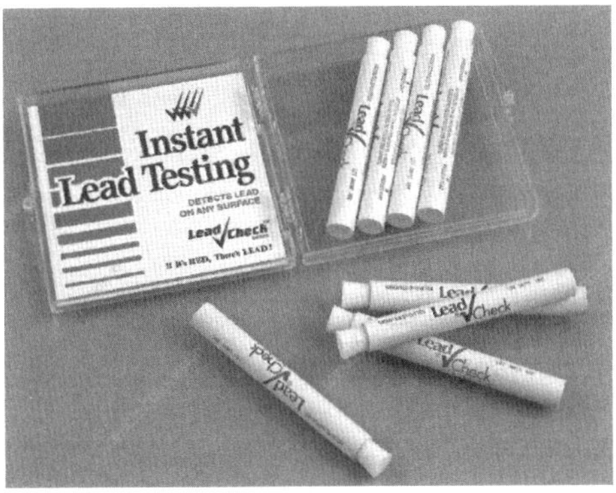

Packaging: After

Packaging that went into Home Depot and Lowe's. Note Joe Moriarty's hand in layout.

Means Lead."

It was a great story, and the packaging looked fantastic—even if some of it was homemade. "We were going so fast that we didn't have time to organize a photo shoot the way you would," says Moriarty. "We needed a hand model to hold the product for the piece of display cardboard in the new packaging. I grabbed the product and said I'd do it myself. If you walk into Home Depot today and buy a LeadCheck test, that's still my hand on the box."

The entire rebranding process was a whirlwind—a matter of weeks to change the logo, the packaging, the infographics, and educational materials on the website; and to recast the advertising from the minimally distributed, text-heavy, black-and-white stuff they had done before. And we did it with a minimal budget—even Joe's hands modeled for free.

It all came together and looked great. But then it was time to roll the dice. LeadCheck could ramp up infrastructure and find more suppliers to try to support bigger volume, but it would mean a lot of capital investment. If demand dropped—either because a competitor got approved or a giant like 3M got into the game—the company would be on the hook for a lot of expensive contracts.

To expand production, LeadCheck arranged for outside funding. Within three months, sales had gone from $500,000 to $10 million. The leadership group got a call from 3M to come to its headquarters in St. Paul, Minnesota, to talk about a potential acquisition.

"I fly out with Marcia, and they bring us into a beautiful

conference room," says Joe. "They show us a video about the history of 3M, and tell us these great stories about how their scientists are free to spend 15 percent of their time independently innovating."

After a break for lunch, as Moriarty remembers, the bad cop took over from the good cop. "A vice president came in and never even sat down. He said, we can manufacture your product tomorrow, and do it for a fraction of the price. He then led us out onto the floor and pointed out the machine that made our blister packaging, and another one that made our ampules, and another that made the tips. He said, we know your patent is up soon, and we're ready to start right now to put you out of business. So, we can work together and come up with what we think is a fair price, or go for option number two."

LeadCheck didn't have the strongest leverage, but as they negotiated the terms of the acquisition, the value of updating the brand became clear. 3M knew it was getting a plug-and-play solution to fill a niche. The EPA approvals, branding, packaging, and performance of the product itself were all in order. 3M had a built-in team of lawyers, accountants, and researchers who could grind out the due diligence and make sure they were buying exactly what they thought they were. After an excruciating 60 days of financial, procedural, and environmental audits, 3M's lawyers signed off on the deal, pushed a button, and transferred enough cash that Dr. Stone would never have to work another day in her life. 3M then shut down the office in Massachusetts and moved the production

When Lightning Strikes

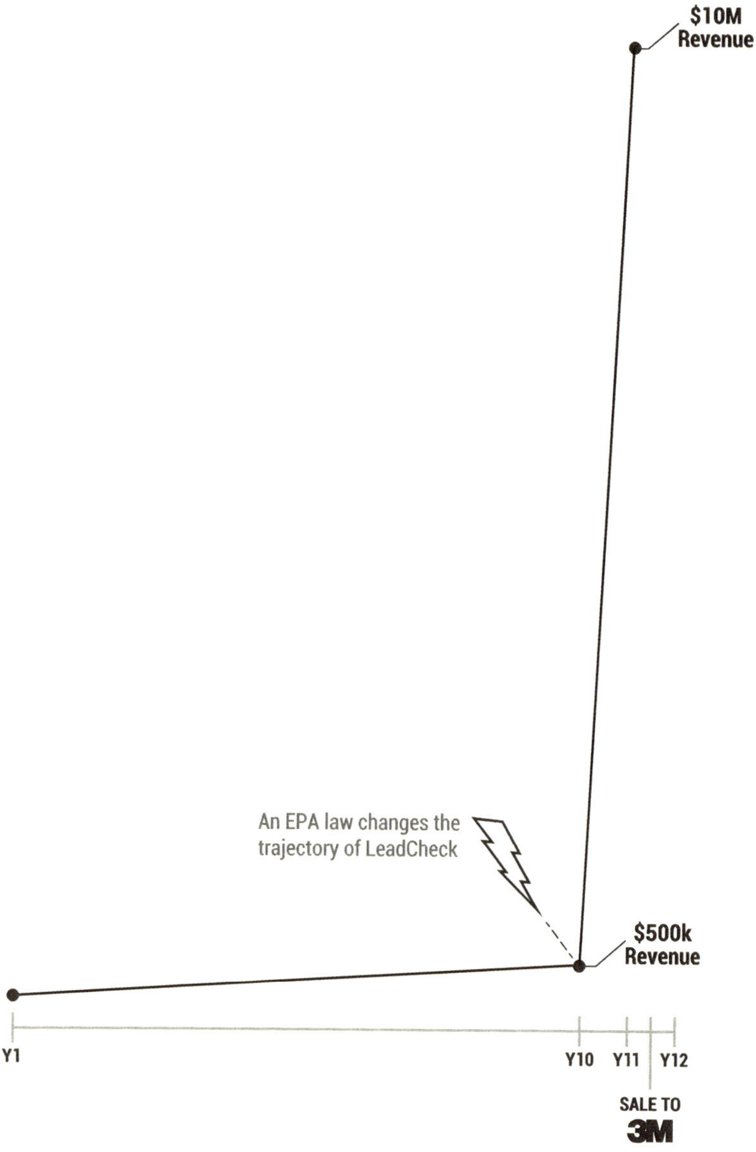

LeadCheck experienced cryptocurrency-like growth in less than a year, with revenues increasing by a multiple of 20 in less than a year.

in-house, to Minnesota—a bittersweet reminder that "exit" really can mean "exit."

LeadCheck got out at exactly the right time. "They don't pay big multiples on manufacturing," says Joe. "If you can take away an acquirer's ability to say, hey, we have to redo all of this packaging, or, we have to go and get all this permitting, you're adding value. What's the validation on what Ted Schlueter did? 3M bought us and put us on the market and didn't change a thing. It still looks exactly the same today."

Let's talk about what you can take away from this case, and apply it to your situation.

Follow the market.

Whenever I have initial consultations with entrepreneurs to see about working together, I start with some specific questions about the market. Many times, I'll get a quick answer accompanied by a wave-off: "There's nobody doing what we do," or "We've found a brand new space." Other times, I'll get a blood-and-guts description of a direct competitor who is the big, obvious challenger in the space. What I'm really hoping for is an honest, clear-eyed assessment of the landscape. I like it when a CEO is angry that he or she hasn't been able to differentiate the company from its nearest competitors. It means he or she is ready to do something about it.

What sorts of questions really get at what your market is?

Who is buying what you're selling? What are they not buying because they picked you? If your thing is relatively unique, what are the substitutes and alternatives and work-arounds that become viable if you get to be too expensive or too unreliable?

What does the mergers-and-acquisitions and venture capital activity look like in your space? Are there other companies coming in? Being sold? Closing down? If an investment banker looked at your last 24 months of financials and your business plan for the next 24 months, what would he or she say?

Joe Moriarty moved on to start Raven360—a company that provides virtual training modules to more than 50 clients and a million individual users. Joe's the co-founder and CEO and his radar is tuned this way: "It isn't just what other training software providers are coming in and out of the space. It's, what is Microsoft doing? What is Salesforce.com doing? What is Amazon Web Services doing?" says Moriarty. "How do you fulfill a potential need? How do you sell something they can't?"

Make the strategic plan.

As we've been mentioning in every one of these chapters, financials are just the lowest common denominator. Everybody has those. The companies that create some separation are ones that are much more sensitive to specifically what has gone right (and wrong) over the last 12 months, and are plotting about what the next 12 to 24 months will look like if things go unexpectedly well, go as predicted, or go poorly.

This means so much more than "We want to double our sales in a year," or "We want to get our product into Target."

What are the actual playbooks you're going to produce and follow to reach your projections? Every section of your business has its own playbook.

What's in your *strategy* playbook? Who are your current and potential partners, suppliers, and clients? What risks are out there surrounding those relationships?

What does your *marketing* playbook look like? For some clients, I operate as almost a surrogate marketing department, grafted onto the corporate structure for a certain term to get that playbook conceived, vetted, and put into operation. For others, I'll work as a fractional chief marketing officer, wading into a project with the company's full-time staff already in place. In both cases, my goal is to infuse some of these best practices into that playbook. What are you going to do with branding? What marketing channels work the best? Which ones haven't shown any return? How are you measuring return on investment?

How is your *engineering* playbook? What does that process look like, specifically? At Joe's company, they use two-week sprints. The engineers get the requirement for a certain feature that needs to be live for a training seminar, and they build for two weeks. After that, it's checked twice and put into production. Then, Joe's engineering team has a specific set of key performance indicators that measure if the module operated the way it was supposed to.

A *sales* playbook is so important because it works for you on separate but parallel tracks. "I don't think a lot of entrepreneurs understand the true value of having not just a set of projections, but a defined system to follow to get there," says Moriarty. "In our sales playbook, we have what the sale process looks like from step one to step 57. Those processes are engineered specifically to get the outcome you want, and you're showing you can bring a new salesperson on board and train them in a repeatable way so they can go out and execute."

The sales playbook is something you can hold up to a potential acquirer, and it's adding value for an exit, but it's also making your day-to-day processes better. Your salespeople are better trained and more likely to be successful, so you're growing your revenue—another thing that adds tangible value.

In Moriarty's opinion, "It's an interesting dance to do, because when you're sitting with a potential investor or somebody who could be interested in acquiring you, they want to hear the speech about how you plan to dominate your market and become this huge, successful company. But what they really want to see when they look under the hood is that you have goals you set, and a predictable process for getting to those goals. It isn't random."

You're showing that there's lots of meat left on the bone—and all they have to do is come and get it.

Seek expertise.

Being an entrepreneur myself, I know the feeling of isolation you can get when you're in the early stages and trying to ride out the hurricane. There are so many decisions to make and fires to put out, and you're the person (by default) who's responsible for all those jobs. Of course, that's a big part of why we do what we do—but that combination of isolation and self-confidence can lead to some errors of omission.

It's impossible to see everything and catch everything, and the reality is that we all have different skill sets. Creative people create, coders code, and engineers engineer.

This is all a short way of saying that an entrepreneur needs to be open to that second set of eyes. As Joe says about LeadCheck, when the phones are ringing and you're trying to solve problems that could threaten the business's existence, you need a set of eyes that is looking over the treeline or down the road.

One of the important roles I play for a client is a fresh set of eyes with no built-in bias, positive or negative, toward a brand or a marketing plan. I don't have the soft spot for something a founder might because of his or her history, and I'm not the person who has thousands of hours invested into a part of the business that should really have lower priority, because another segment has a more attractive potential market.

We're all human, and some of that information is tough to swallow. You might avoid dealing with it all yourself. Every one of the CEOs and leaders I've worked with in the real world and used for these cases is a part of an elaborate, interconnected web of mentors and mentees, so they can ask the right questions and provide answers for other people in earlier stages who are looking for guidance.

Using consultants and other outside experts who have very specific, demonstrable expertise and success in their category is a way to hack the development process. It saves time and it saves money, because it shortens the route you have to take around the track.

Don't sell. Get bought.

It might seem like a semantic difference, but selling and getting bought are different things when it comes to an exit.

As Joe described, LeadCheck was in a full-blast fire drill to create rebranding, sales channels, packaging, supplier relationships—basically everything you need to be a functioning entity. When it came time to meet with 3M, LeadCheck was obviously not in the driver's seat, so it sold to 3M.

"A potential acquirer wants to see an organization that is well run, with all the documentation in place. What does the HR process look like? What are the playbooks we were talking about before?" Moriarty says. "There's a lot of value in how you do things, and how you can show they're repeatable. That's where the increased multiples come from—from acquirers recognizing that you're not only doing things at a high level, but you can replicate it."

By establishing those guideposts and systems ahead of time, you're not only setting yourself up to get bought, and have more leverage in those conversations. You're also making it much less nerve-racking to operate in the high-speed, high-stress environment that is the 21st-century marketplace. Your speed and ability to adapt and pivot are being baked into your business model.

CHAPTER 5

Orchestrate and Automate: What Are You Selling?

If you ever saw Pulp Fiction, *you might remember Harvey Keitel as The Wolf. In the business world, The Wolf is Mike Torto, minus the gangster spin. When it comes to tough situations, he's "the cleaner." He's brought in as a CEO who knows how to take an engine, rip out the bad wires, and rebuild it while it's running. He's no BS and a straight shooter, and he totally believes in marketing and "appropriately disruptive" thinking. His charge to me was simple: stop the Embotics company from selling "feature-and-function bingo" to low-level IT decision makers, and start selling solutions to CTOs and CEOs. Twenty-four months later, Embotics was sold to Swedish company Snow for a significant multiple.*

Mike Torto is a fixer.

If you're in private equity and you've invested in a company that isn't performing the way you want, Mike is the one who parachutes in, turns it around, and positions it for the next move. He has a long and distinguished track record in B-to-B tech, leading a half-dozen companies to successful (and profitable) exits.

Our paths crossed for the first time in 2017, after Mike had been called in to figure out a way to get cloud-management company Embotics to realize the potential that got its private-equity investors interested in it in the first place.

The "cloud" is everywhere today, but in the early 2010s, it wasn't much more than a concept. Embotics' founders figured there would come a time when organizations with big digital infrastructure needs like NASA or NTT Data would get out of the business of building and maintaining those servers, networks, and interfaces themselves, and rely on an outside vendor to not only provide infrastructure but also maintain it. It's a space Amazon Web Services has come to dominate, but back in 2012, Amazon was still mostly an online bookseller.

Embotics was one of the earliest companies to be among these "cloud dashboard" providers, but had struggled to push beyond a million dollars in revenue. "When you saw other companies like CloudBolt really start to take off in such an important category, you had to say, what are they doing that we aren't?" says Torto. "When I got the call from the existing investors to take a look, I saw a number of issues, from how the company was capitalized, how it was positioning itself, and how they were trying to serve their target markets. They were all over the place. As the wind blew, they would pivot and try to change strategies or develop something very specific for you, and then very specific for the next company and the next company, just to get revenue through the door."

Mike had a problem with a lot of moving parts. Embotics had spent the past five years lurching around, trying to find the right market position. It had put itself up for sale two other times, with no success. Revenue was flat, and the investors were approaching a decade in this company. It was time to figure out the end—an exit, or, if it couldn't be sold, just shutting it down.

When we got together, in late 2017, everything was on the table. How could Embotics reposition itself *again* without it looking like more of the same—and producing more of the same market indifference? How could it organize the services it provided into easier-to-understand (and sell) solutions and platforms instead of a menu of individual services that didn't stand out in the market, were time intensive, and didn't produce much margin? The most drastic possibility, short of closing the doors for good, was changing the company's name. Changing the logo on the website doesn't even approach how expensive and fraught with risk a name change is. It involves changing everything internally and externally, and coming up with an entirely new story to tell your clients, suppliers, and internal team. It's a massive, expensive step to take, and one most companies and their investors don't have the stomach for. And in this case, that kind of investment would really have been a waste, since our thesis was the most likely buyer would come from outside the United States, where the company didn't have a lot of name recognition anyway.

I decided to do some digging into what Embotics was already doing, to see if there might be a simpler path forward. After several months talking to current and potential customers in the space, it became clear that single-track solutions weren't particularly useful for large-enterprise customers. The chief technology officer at one of those companies has two branches of the same tree under him or her. On one side, you have the IT department, which is extremely risk-averse and wants predictable, repeatable solutions. I like to call it the Department of "No."

On the other side, you have the development teams, which are the Wild West. They're the Department of "Never Mind the Money." They want to try a bunch of things, charge it all on the credit card, and throw it up on the cloud to see what works and what doesn't.

For Embotics to create some traction, it needed to position itself as a single global solution for the CTO and those two competing interests down the chain. I needed to help Mike figure out how to talk to different audiences with one voice but in multiple dialects.

Embotics could automate digital business processes cleanly and reliably. For example, a new hire could log into his or her computer, get set up with security and compliance, and be working on the cloud within an hour. That was the easy part—the price of admission in that space, and something

Making the Maestro

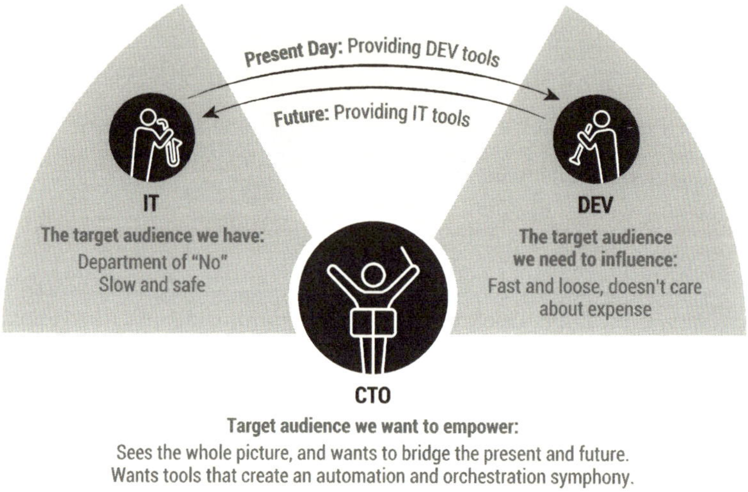

Present Day: Providing DEV tools
Future: Providing IT tools
IT
The target audience we have:
Department of "No"
Slow and safe
DEV
The target audience we need to influence:
Fast and loose, doesn't care about expense
CTO
Target audience we want to empower:
Sees the whole picture, and wants to bridge the present and future.
Wants tools that create an automation and orchestration symphony.

Embotics needed to tell the story of how it could make IT decision makers the internal "maestros" of their organization, with better tools to manage the push and pull between daily operations and development.

Embotics had done for clients like GE. But Embotics could also *orchestrate*—provide the vast, flexible resources a development team would need to move projects back and forth at speed, and create dedicated, secure areas for those teams to run repetitions and experiment.

The analogy we created for this platform effect was from the world of music. In an orchestra, the conductor (the *maestro,* to be precise) runs the show, and needs to simultaneously manage the string section (IT) and the woodwinds (development team).

Embotics would provide the platform (or stage!) to perform in concert.

We created the tagline, "Let the symphony begin."

All of those CTOs and heads of IT and development have egos, and they all want to think of themselves as maestros. With Embotics, they all could be. It was an empowering message, and a very human one. There was no tech jargon or laundry list of the bells and whistles that made the platform go. It was strictly conceptualizing and describing the feeling of working together in harmony.

The goal was to gain mindshare with the specific group of decision makers who would understand how Embotics could streamline their digital business processes. I knew that the crowd at the annual VM World trade show would be primed for this message. We hired a string quartet to represent the "symphony" Embotics would help a CTO conduct. Using the show's volume restrictions as a benefit instead of a limitation, we had the quartet play "silently" (the only way to hear the music was through headsets at the booth). It was engaging content and generated a tremendous amount of buzz through the show.

The issue for Embotics wasn't the ability to solve a client's problems. That, they could do, even if it was piecemeal. What this research and this campaign did was discover what the decision makers in the market wanted and needed, and reframed what Embotics did to scratch that itch.

The story Embotics began to tell resonated not only with customers, but also with international strategic buyers who had been poking around the space to see if there was a way to bolt new functionality onto their current stack.

"I had interviewed and started with seven different investment bankers, competing to get my business to sell the company," recalls Torto. "They went out on their own and asked different people in private equity, venture capital, and potential strategic buyers if they had heard of Embotics. None of them had. But those bankers could never get anybody to the next step, which was, why should they be interesting to me? The first company that came along after this campaign was Flexera—a company I had never heard of because they were in a completely different area called license management. What that did is help us go in and say, okay, who else in that space should care about what we're doing? How do you then target them and create a sense of urgency?"

Torto frames that sense of urgency as the difference between being a "nice to have" and a "need to have." A "nice to have" might turn into a straightforward sale, or produce a meeting with that CTO from the trade show or another department head about a potential partnership. A "need to have" moves *up* the food chain, not just down. It means the C-level executives are suddenly paying attention to a company that could be an integral part of its future.

"Before Embotics, I had a company called Centive that was in the sales commission automation space," says Torto. "We built an application that let you automate commission plans for sales reps. It let a company get commissioned sales programs right so that finance and sales were aligned. That way, salespeople weren't getting frustrated and quitting because they didn't earn enough for their sales, and companies weren't forced to let overcompensated salespeople go because they had to bring in cheaper people. It dawned on me that that was a nice feature, but the only way to attract a really big player would be to show how it could integrate into one of the general compensation companies like Paychex or ADP as a part of what they did every day."

Torto had spent two years building a low-level partnership between Centive and ADP—which is headquartered off I-280 in Roseland, New Jersey. He also knew that one of ADP's vice presidents (responsible for $2 billion in business) commuted on the New Jersey Turnpike to get to work. So Torto put up a billboard on the turnpike touting the partnership between the two companies. He got a call from that vice president shortly after the billboard went up. "They didn't know exactly what we were before, and after that 'stealth move,' they did. And bingo, you're in their head."

In hockey, the difference between an ordinary second-line center and star center Wayne Gretzky is the ability to not go where the play is, but to go where the play is going to be. For Embotics, the play was going to be an international buyer, because that market in the cloud space was a year or two behind where the United States market was—and international buyers were less likely to care about the stigma of a company that hadn't sold the last two times it went on the block. "I had given my initial list of who I thought were the most natural buyers from within my space," says Torto. "What I didn't know was that there was a Swedish company out there that had to dramatically change the way they were going to market, and even though they were small, they went out and got private-equity capital to do acquisitions so they could market cloud infrastructure management. Because we had flooded the market with what our capability was, they had learned about us. Without a branding-for-buyout strategy, that never would have happened."

As we discussed with the Etonic case, looking beyond the backyard for potential buyers opened up a whole new world (literally), and ultimately left open the ability to be more flexible in what tools could be used to position the brand. The expanded buyer pool only knew what we were broadcasting as a part of our new messaging. We didn't have to spend the time and money to deal with any scar tissue that was left in the American market.

That Swedish company, Snow Software, bought Embotics in 2019. The deal closed at an enviable multiple, and the two companies built a close relationship very early in the acquisition process. Torto attributes these to the one-two punch of an investment bank (AGC) at the peak of its powers, and a branding-and-research ground game that told the right story at the right time. "Because we did the work ahead of time, we had time to understand the players and what they cared about and what their emotional buy-in was," says Torto. "There was an emotional connection, not just a financial one. That's just as important of a tool as anything else you can use."

What are you really selling?

Another company Mike Torto consults on operates in the construction management space. It uses automated sensors to determine work conditions in warehouses—if there are spills on the floor, too much carbon monoxide in the air, or a slate of other environmental concerns. The company started out trying to innovate the technology behind the sensors, but it quickly became apparent that value wasn't in reinventing the wheel, but in using cheaper, off-the-shelf sensors that could already do the job, and integrating them with the company's easy-to-use monitoring platform. "Those aren't always the easiest questions to ask yourself—what really is driving value here?—because the answers can make you have to make some hard choices," says Torto. "But I'm always looking for the way to take something that exists, repurpose it, and drive more value from the same technology."

It's always about the money.

Since we're talking about value, let's talk about cash.

Some entrepreneurs don't think they're ever going to sell their business because it's a life passion, or because they envision passing it down to their children like their parents did to them.

I get all of that.

And yes, not every company is destined to be bought out by a competitor or a private-equity group.

But.

Whether you want to admit it or not, the point of doing the work—and putting in the thousands and thousands of hours—is to make money. It's to make a living. It's to build something that has value. You want to create that value for yourself or for your family. I understand the sentiment that goes with keeping the money conversation out of it. It sounds more noble to say you want to grow something that can save the world.

All of those things together can be true!

My point is that if you're going to do this, you might as well do it in a way that maximizes your options. When you build your company using the principles in this book, it will be more attractive to potential buyers and worth more money—whether you end up selling it or not. That's valuable for a lot of reasons. It's valuable if you ever want to get a mortgage for a house, or a loan for your business. It makes it easier to find investors who will help you reach more of the world. It provides a framework to make decisions, both day-to-day and strategically.

It also has the benefit of giving you some signals about when to stop. Stopping can mean exiting because somebody wants to buy you out. It can mean transferring some responsibilities to other people, because your role as a leader or a rainmaker is too time-consuming to be preoccupied with paperwork. Or it can mean a better understanding of when it's time to close the doors.

Knowledge is power, and knowing where you stand at all times is the best surveillance money can buy.

Make visualization a habit.

Talking about visualization might seem a little abstract for some people, but if you eavesdrop on the world of elite athletes and coaches, it's something you hear all the time. People win Olympic medals and world titles and qualify for the Navy SEALs because they are not only well trained, but they intentionally visualize what they expect to happen.

Now, visualizing is different than dreaming. Anybody can lay back and think about winning the lottery or having six-pack abs or throwing the game-winning touchdown pass in the Super Bowl. What visualization does is connect the real-world training and preparation you're doing with what you expect the outcome to be from that training.

One of the most vivid descriptions of it comes from golf champion Tiger Woods when he talks about his putting. He matches each putt to the picture he sees in his head. He's hit thousands of putts in his career, and the visualization is essentially a home movie of what his brain predicts is going to happen with the one he has in front of him now—because he knows subconsciously that he's seen a putt a lot like it thousands of times before.

Of course, the foundation of Tiger's visualization is that he actually experienced all those other putts. Now is your opportunity to keep adding to your own bank of experiences, and making sure you're fully prepared for all the contingencies you could face. When you can do the mental repetitions ahead of time—playing in the what-if space—you're essentially practicing your response ahead of the fact. "I wrote myself a check for a hundred million dollars and I keep it taped to the door at my home office," says Torto. "It's not a dream. It's my every day, whether it's building a partnership or going to market or figuring out how to sell something or building a brand or building value. It's the same thing a golfer does in the last round of a tournament, or a basketball player who needs to make the free throw with three seconds left on the clock. I visualize what is going to happen that day. I see myself in the next meeting. I hear myself in a negotiation. I try to anticipate what the objections are going to be that may block me from that outcome, and I see what I'm going to do to be ready for them. We all know people in our lives who talk about doing this or doing that, but don't end up putting in the work because they're afraid it's going to be too hard. And they get blocked."

As you'll learn more about in Chapter 8, when you hear from noted executive coach Dan Guglielmo, seeing and *feeling* your future actually help create a new mental pathway that pushes the older, less productive pathways to the side. Like Chevy Chase's Ty Webb says in *Caddyshack,* you really can be your future.

CHAPTER 6

Thinking Bigger: Branding into the Future

PopCorners makes all-natural corn chips with its proprietary compression-popping process, and after gaining some traction in the Northeast, they were trying to establish the brand nationally. I had done lots of work with my friend (and superstar brand strategist) Meredith McPherron before, and she introduced me to PopCorners CEO Paul Nardone at a board meeting for the Governor's Academy prep school. Paul doesn't beat around the bush. He told me that if I could come up with a successful plan for the school's branding and capital campaign, I could have a shot at the PopCorners business. Deal.

Junk food was having an identity crisis in the early 2010s. It used to be that millions of consumers were willing to spend billions of dollars to shovel as much junk food as they could into their mouths in the form of sugary candy, chemical-laden snack chips, and processed "meals" that came in a box with a plastic toy.

You can still find whatever kind of Doritos you like at the gas station, but the biggest snack manufacturers are realizing that the market is looking for healthier alternatives. The global "healthy snacks" market is expected to increase by $25 billion by 2027—a bump of almost 40 percent.

The Goldman Sachs research department produced a hugely influential mini-documentary in 2019 called *The Snack Attack,* which defined not only the trend toward healthier snack foods with premium ingredients, but a fundamental change in how Americans ate meals. A lot of us aren't doing the three-squares-a-day thing anymore, and on-the-go salty "mini-meals" have filled the void. The Goldman team finished the report by emphasizing that global companies, both inside and outside the traditional snack business, were looking for ways to stay abreast of that trend.

Those facts by themselves could have put PopCorners in an advantageous position, but the brand hadn't capitalized on them. Now it was time to do something.

Paul Nardone came to BFY Brands (parent of PopCorners) with a glittering track record as a consumer packaged-goods operator. As CEO of Annie's Homegrown from 1993 to 2004, he led the team responsible for growing that brand from a charming local delicacy sold out of an unheated barn in Connecticut into a genuine challenger to Kraft macaroni and cheese. After Annie's sold to a private-equity group, Paul went on to lead exits for Stirrings cocktail mixers to international beverage giant Diageo, and for Immaculate Baking ready-to-bake cookies to General Mills.

By 2015, he had been brought in by BFY's private-equity owners to work some of the same magic for PopCorners—and catch the eye of some of the players in Big Food. "I came in with my eye already on finding the right strategic buyers, because the rewards would be more profound for our shareholders," says Paul. "I came in with a set of key things I wanted to bring to life to make that happen."

The first was to change the space PopCorners played in. "PopCorners wasn't positioned as a premium, natural product," he says. "It was a conventional corn product—and I thought that was the wrong positioning. More than 95 percent of the U.S. corn crop is genetically modified, and I said we need to be on the other side of that, because that's where the market is going."

Hand in hand with that was proving the brand could create a national footprint in the "natural" channel—and get into chains like Whole Foods Markets and Sprouts. "It's not so much getting deep into all the channels, but proving what you can do in each of them—so you're leaving something on the table for the big strategic to come and invest heavily in," says Paul. "If we hadn't gotten into Whole Foods or a single Walmart or Target, it would have been hard to get the proper inputs to extrapolate what that could potentially be worth."

The stark reality of the consumer packaged-goods space is that the biggest players have massive research-and-development teams and virtually unlimited resources—like 3M in a previous chapter. A company like Pepsi or Nestle can create and produce any product it wants. For PopCorners to resonate, it needed to be a differentiated brand that spoke to consumers and was hard to replicate. Essentially, it'd be easier for a big company to buy the whole thing than build something to compete with it. "If they thought they could easily make it themselves," says Paul, "why would they buy it from you?"

Paul first learned that lesson when he started at Annie's. In one of his first weeks at the company, he visited a local supermarket with Andrew Martin, one of the co-founders and then-chairman—who had co-founded Smartfood popcorn before leaving and adapting the Smartfood cheese to pasta shells. "We stood in front of this 12-foot section of boxed pasta meals—a billion-and-a-half-dollar category—and there was one box of Annie's in the whole 12-foot section," Paul recalls. "I was young and coming up and trying to eat healthy myself, and I thought there was room in this big market for a healthy alternative. I drew the same parallel to other adjacent categories—SpaghettiOs, Hamburger Helper, PastaRoni. It was virgin space in the sense that there were no other natural brands in these very large, very tired categories. It was starving for provocative innovation, and it could begin at a place where it was smaller than something the big guys would even bother to pay attention to."

Fast forward to PopCorners, when Paul decided to train the company's sights specifically on the healthy-snack space, he started by building a new team. First, he brought in Meredith McPherron as a strategic advisor to direct the repositioning of the brand. At the time, Meredith was a venture partner at Glasswing Ventures and an active investor in several angel syndicates. Previously she had run the Rock Center for Entrepreneurship at Harvard Business School and had experience with several start-ups, as well as major names General Mills, Guinness Import Company, and Goldman Sachs—putting her in rare company as an executive with marketing, enterprise, and entrepreneurial experience. She is now the CEO and managing partner of Drive by DraftKings, a sports tech/entertainment venture-capital firm founded by DraftKings, General Catalyst, Accomplice, and Boston Seed Capital.

Paul and I met because he happened to be on the board of Governor's Academy, an independent prep school north of Boston, and he and Meredith were co-chairing a capital campaign for the school. Meredith and I had worked together on projects for years before she brought me in to help with a campaign for Governor's. Paul and I hit it off, and it became my mission to work with Meredith and PopCorners' small, in-house marketing team to fundamentally change the market's perception of what PopCorners was—and the ways the company could measure the response.

The concept Meredith developed was centered on "Do One Better." PopCorners would not be just a chip, but a small (and meaningful) decision anyone could make to do something more positive and beneficial—for their health, for the environment. It was as natural as seeing the elevator in front of you, but deciding to take the stairs.

Part of the work in repositioning the brand was to encourage consumers to differentiate PopCorners from the other choices and to latch onto it. The chips are genuinely delicious—not just something you tolerate because Doritos aren't in your diet. They're low-calorie, gluten free, nut free, and have no trans fats, no artificial flavors or colors, and no preservatives. They even come in a variety of flavors. The corn in the chips is sourced entirely from independent family farms that follow strict quality control and guidelines to meet Non-GMO Verification Certification. It's an easy brand to feel good about.

But telling the story successfully to the consumer was only part of the job. "Lots of companies can achieve product-market fit," says Meredith. "They might not need to see how the sausage is made, so to speak. But being able to show how the sausage is made *at the right time* can have a lot of value to an acquiring company. As a company scales, it's wise to consider the market of potential acquiring companies, and how the company will learn and understand more about its own potential."

This branding of a company's future state takes different forms than the traditional things you might see in an investment banker's toolkit. In previous generations, a company like BFY Brands would be discovered by a potential acquirer, and the banker would present a set of financials and there'd be a bland PowerPoint deck made up. It would then be up to the people in the room to sell these dry pieces as an accurate representation of what the company was.

Paul, Meredith, and I did something totally different. We wanted to capture the fact that PopCorners had a marketing engine that was working 24 hours a day, engaging with customers—talking to them, wooing them. We wanted to show the vibrancy of the brand, and reinforce the scope of PopCorners' contribution to the healthy-snack lifestyle and its potential to dominate the category.

We made a 60-second hype video that covered everything from the brand's commitment to the small, organic farmers who grew the non-GMO corn, to the dedicated production facilities that took extra care to make sure the food met every quality standard. The JetBlue airline offered PopCorners on its flights, so we Photoshopped a PopCorners wrap on a JetBlue plane. We showed the brand as a way for consumers to make the simple choice to Do One Better every day, and as a way for the future owner to use the inroads Paul and his team had established to supercharge market penetration. "It showed the roots of the brand and what was possible, but in a way that was tangible and real," says Meredith. "It generated an energy that said, I want to be a part of this thing."

If you've ever seen a Confidential Investment Memorandum (CIM), you know they aren't rocket science. They're designed to make you understand the financial picture. In an auction with an in-demand company selling to a handful of motivated buyers, it's essentially an owner's manual. But for the vast majority of potential transactions, the potential and the boundaries—and even the potential players—aren't always so clear. What we're doing—and what you need to be considering in your own situation—is how to extract and reveal all the value that could be obscured within those financials.

"What you're doing is sending signals to get attention beyond the 'growth' numbers," says Meredith. "When you looked at what PopCorners did, the trajectory of the business fundamentally changed with the repositioning, and that story needed to be told along with the one about the quality of the assets—great distribution and an amazing supply chain and a culture of discipline and sustainability."

Pepsi had gone on a spree of acquisitions in the "healthy" space to bolster its "Winning with Purpose" program—an initiative to promote community and planet health. It spent more than $3 billion to buy SodaStream, the maker of in-home carbonated beverage machines, Bare baked fruit snacks, and Health Warrior plant-based nutrition bars. And in December 2019, it finished a six-month period of due diligence and acquired PopCorners for a very large undisclosed sum.

The next time you shop, you'll still be able to find Doritos, but you'll probably see a bag of PopCorners next to them.

Let's talk about what you can learn from this case.

Brand the future.

What you *are* is clearly important to your day-to-day customers, but you have to have a brand story that tells your customers *why* they should buy your product or service, and

Branding Intent

The story you tell has to go beyond the today and show potential buyers a detailed vision of what you could become in the future.

projects an enticing future that would attract buyout offers. It's no different than an NFL team trading a player for draft picks. The team getting the player sees a way for it to acquire a specific, known skill set (or a construction project it believes it can finish where the previous team failed). The team getting the draft picks sees a more attractive version of its future. Each side works hard to tell the story of what the other side wants and needs. For PopCorners, one way to do that was to reiterate the story of its operational superiority. A potential acquirer wouldn't need to ramp up any special equipment or change its own processes to make the proprietary chips. PopCorners had two production facilities in the northeast and another in Europe. Pepsi knew it would be able to buy the brand and just plug it in after a brief integration. "A lot of folks leave a lot on the table simply because they haven't proven what they say—and if you can't prove it, you can't get credit for it," says

Paul. "Tell the story of what you are and what you could be, and prove that what you have can get it there." Nothing about that process is haphazard or seat-of-the-pants. If you aren't intentionally building and polishing your *brand intent*—a full-color description and story about what your brand *could be in the future,* you're leaving unrealized value.

Don't be afraid of change.

As the world of business analytics becomes more sophisticated, so does the available array of key performance indicators. You can measure virtually everything, which also means you can *look* at everything if you're so inclined.

Building the appropriate dashboard could fill another book, but Paul shares an important point here: "You want to have access to enough data to make informed decisions, but smaller, early-stage companies need to take advantage of their ability to be fast-moving. You can play with all the analytical tools the big companies play with, but if that causes you to behave the same way they behave, you've lost your advantage."

You have to separate the ability to assemble meaningful information from the ability to digest it, draw conclusions, and make decisions. Paul recalls, "With PopCorners, we made some mistakes with the products we brought to market. A bigger company with more resources wouldn't put out something without all kinds of market testing. But we went ahead anyway, made those mistakes, and were nimble enough to adapt, learn, and move on from them. A bigger company might use 25 people and a year of analysis to make a decision, which makes the stakes for that decision much higher, and it takes much longer to change course. But that's only an advantage if you're willing to take it."

Find an evangelist.

The LeadCheck case from a previous chapter reinforced what can happen when large companies are involved in acquiring a niche player. The experience can be relatively impersonal, with meetings between people who only know each other by email signature.

But in a world of big data, interpersonal skills still matter. Forging a relationship with somebody "in the room" can give you an ally throughout the process. Even if that doesn't translate specifically into better deal terms, it can help navigate some of the complexities more efficiently. "You need somebody on the management team who is willing to raise their hand and say, I want to sponsor this," says Paul. "When somebody internally is willing to go to bat for you, it's like having somebody turn on the lights and show you where the boxes are you need to check."

The same advice holds true within the world of investment banking. An honest, two-way relationship with a good I-banker is like swimming with an extra set of legs. "When you have an investment banker who is truly a partner, that person helps you think critically about the process, and how to address any push-back that comes from the meetings you have," Paul observes. "There's a lot of reasons deals don't get done. A good investment banker will help navigate the deal so those reasons don't become an issue."

In Chapter 8, we're going to talk more about the role investment bankers play.

Expand and adapt.

Entrepreneurs who have never been through an exit should have the tools to competently approach one from a brand point of view. But experience is its own teacher—provided you're willing to listen and take notes.

Paul was essentially learning the art of the exit in real time at Annie's, as he navigated his way through the exit process—which actually spread over several years as he both pitched the company to strategic buyers and listened to offers from private-equity groups who were interested in investing. "Being in those big conference rooms and presenting to the president of a division or the CEO of a business and having the entire management team in there listening, it gave me real experience in how the game was played," Paul remembers. "I didn't even really understand what would happen next. But by the time I got to my next exit and then the next one, I got better at understanding what points I needed to hammer home."

Accumulating his own experience was one piece, but Paul also wasn't shy about asking for insight from experienced mentors: "Back during the early Annie's days, we didn't even have access to the syndicated data that showed how our brand was doing in stores. It was just too expensive for us to get. You could either be completely in the dark, or you could beg and borrow from people you know in the business to try to get the information you need. There's nothing wrong about being clueless about things when you start out, but you want to be a sponge and learn from the people who have been in the business for 30 years. Today, I'm one of those 30-year guys. I took a call from a young entrepreneur just now, and I enjoy those moments because it makes me reflect back to my humble days. I want to help, because I was fortunate to get help when I was coming up."

Solving the Acquisition Puzzle

PopCorners as a salty snack
Gets lost in PepsiCo's vast snack portfolio

PopCorners as a better-for-you snack
Fills a previously underserved space in that portfolio

PepsiCo was looking to enter the better-for-you snack space. Had PopCorners continued to sell itself as a salty snack, it would have gotten lost among all of PepsiCo's holdings—and would not have been a natural fit for acquisition.

CHAPTER 7

Two Deals, Not One: Can You Live with It?

Dick Emerson is a rare guy. A renaissance man in the truest sense of the term. He's been my boss, a mentor, and a friend. He's someone who understands life—the good and the bad. He rode through the last of the Mad Men era, albeit with extreme integrity. After selling his own small agency to Boston's Arnold Worldwide, he went on to facilitate a dozen acquisitions for the company, which went on to achieve the auspicious title "Agency of the World."

If 3M gives you an ultimatum like they did with LeadCheck—and says they'll bury you if you don't make a deal—the choices in front of you aren't exactly choices. Entrepreneurship doesn't work like that. It's a series of judgment calls: gut reactions backed up with some data. Sometimes, it's being faced with a menu of imperfect options, making your selection, and trying to make it fit after the fact.

The last thing I want to do is sell you on the idea that your exit experience will be linear and clean and perfect.

It won't.

It'll be like a war. You'll win some battles and lose some battles, and through both you'll be trying to achieve the overall objective without getting too bloodied or discouraged. I'm going to talk about a case in this chapter, but it'll be slightly different than previous ones because I didn't participate as a consultant.

My friend Dick Emerson is a legend in the branding and advertising business. He's had a long career as a founding partner in his own ad agency (Emerson Lane Fortuna) and as a managing partner for advertising giant Arnold Worldwide. You might not know Arnold by name, but you know the work. That's the agency that came up with the familiar "Drivers Wanted" campaign for Volkswagen, the "Body Bag" anti-smoking ad for the American Legacy Foundation—which they executed in tandem with Crispin Porter & Bogusky—and the "Flo" campaign for Progressive Insurance.

Dick has a long track record helping brands successfully become more human and relatable. He has also gone through his own exit, and has consulted with creative organizations going through the same process. He sold his agency to Arnold in 1991, and after leaving that company in 2000, he became a partner at Toth + Co, the Boston creative agency famous for its work with Tommy Hilfiger and with Taylor Swift's Keds campaign.

When you hear how Dick's first agency—Emerson Lane Fortuna—originated, it will probably resonate with your entrepreneurial heart. "We were three guys with big-agency experience—a marketer, a writer, and an art director. We figured we could offer the big-agency experience without the big-agency overhead," Dick says. "We started this agency from nothing, in 1981. We had to go to the bank for the $15,000 we needed, and the interest rate was 21 percent. It was, in many ways, the worst possible time to start an agency."

Boston in the early 1980s was a hotbed for creative talent and high tech. Lotus, Digital Equipment Corp., and Wang Laboratories were in their heyday, and employed more than a quarter of a million people around Boston. Emerson could see that the big Boston agencies were engaging in open warfare for the biggest, splashiest tech clients and lavishing big salaries on creative talent to do the work.

That left a gaping hole. Many smaller, less sexy (but highly recognized!) clients were being underserved. "For a time, it seemed like we could stand at ground level at Boston's high-rise agencies, holding big baskets to catch the unhappy clients who floated down from above," recalls Dick. "But we ran into the classic problem. There weren't enough of us to go around.

We only had 100 percent of our *time* to sell."

What had been an agile, low-cost operation started to add staff and functionality. Clients needed public relations to go with their advertising campaigns. Emerson hired for that. Clients wanted a one-stop shop that could push out their campaigns on television. Emerson built a media department.

Ironically, after executing a business plan that called for being the highly experienced, lower-cost alternative to Boston's largest agencies, Emerson Lane Fortuna needed to either acquire some smaller agencies to ramp up growth, or to identify a larger Boston agency that could be the perfect parent. Arnold Advertising was the ideal parental candidate.

Arnold had recently been purchased by Ed Eskandarian—a real-life rocket scientist turned ad man. Eskandarian had a firm grasp of the scientific principles behind mass and lift, and he was applying them to growing his agency. What Arnold lacked was creative cachet. Emerson's agency had just won "Best of Show" at the Hatch Awards—New England's most prestigious creative prize. "I got a call from Ed Eskandarian, and we sat down to talk. He was trying to grow, and I was trying to grow, and we had what he was missing. It was a perfect fit," says Dick.

Making it happen, as Dick remembers, was a huge challenge. He had to get his two other partners on board, and to accept the idea that being subsumed by a larger company meant that it wasn't going to be a merger of equals. The experience taught him a lesson, which he says any entrepreneur can learn much earlier in the life cycle than he did.

"I think you can be the person who approaches an

acquisition from an offensive mindset or a defensive mindset, and those are two totally different kinds of experiences," says Dick. "The person who looks at an acquisition from an offensive standpoint has done a good job managing their business and is looking at it from the standpoint of, how do I improve this? They know that the right fit means that two plus two equals way more than four."

But on the defensive side, the tone is far different. "In that space," says Dick, the attitude is more often, how am I ever going to get my value out of this thing? You're banging your head against the wall, thinking you have to do something. This is one of life's most emotional experiences. It's all the blood, sweat, and tears you put into something. The people who do better have a strong sense of self, a true sense of purpose, and a good sense of humor—because life in this business can get crazy."

Even the best personal equilibrium will be challenged during the course of a potential exit deal because, as the seller, you're in a very vulnerable position. Eskandarian would go on to sell Arnold to direct-mail giant Snyder Communications, and Snyder had even more aggressive and widespread growth plans. The now-subsidiary Arnold sent Dick Emerson to do due diligence on a potential acquisition in Canada, and part of the process was sitting in meetings with that agency's chairman and its three biggest clients to see how they would feel about being serviced by a new, larger agency after an acquisition. It was a delicate set of conversations, because if the clients said they wouldn't stay, it could not only affect the price the company might attract from Arnold, but could cause the deal to cave in. Worse than that, the deal could crater and the Canadian agency's clients could leave, because they were spooked by their partner looking around to make a change.

"The agency chairman even said to the client that they were looking into doing a deal with us so that they could keep up with the client's growth in the future," says Emerson, who helped integrate a dozen acquisitions during his time at Arnold. "I went back and reported my findings, but Arnold's new parent company decided not to go forward. I had sat with this guy and his three largest accounts and sold them the value of this, and for it to go that way was a painful experience for everybody. You need somebody to walk you through these things, as opposed to walking you straight off the plank. When it was clear that Arnold's new parent was calling all the shots, I knew it was time for me to move on."

That's an extreme example, but it tells an important story every entrepreneur needs to know. Dick puts it very well when he says you have to be prepared for all the twists and turns that are inevitably going to come. "One of the interesting things I've seen happen, time and time again, is that the first conversation an entrepreneur has with somebody from the acquiring company, if it's with the head of the company—who often is also an entrepreneur—that's an easy conversation. That produces a lot of optimism. But then the next person in the conversation is the CFO, and he or she is usually Dr. No. His or her job is to find a way to pay as little as possible. So you go from the high to the low pretty fast. That's why the sense of self is so important, and to have people around you who can help you deal with that boiling cauldron of emotions."

Let's look at three of the main takeaways from this case.

Be sure you understand the dynamics of the deal—actually, two deals—before you sign.

You're probably going to have lawyers and accountants walking you through the specifics of the deal you'll sign when you exit, and those terms are going to be concrete. Documents will be signed. Money will change hands. Keys will get passed. But, as Dick likes to say, a deal isn't a deal.

It's two deals.

There's the deal you do—which is the "money changing hands" part. And there's the deal you live after the money changes hands. Many people don't pay enough attention to that. It's part of why Dick decided to eventually leave Arnold after he merged his agency with them. The finances were a match, but the culture wasn't.

From my own vantage point, learning from good friends and mentors in the advertising and marketing business, like Dick and longtime Boston and New York advertising exec Tucker Greco (now sadly deceased), has been like following somebody else through a minefield and learning how to avoid the explosions.

Look in the mirror.

Imagine you're a pilot. One of the most dangerous things that can happen to a pilot is spatial disorientation. That's when what you're registering with your senses doesn't match what's actually happening in the plane. Instead of being able to see the horizon and feel the plane moving up or down or left or right, the signals are confused and you end up steering the plane into the ground or an obstacle.

The stakes aren't quite that high when it comes to an exit, but entrepreneurs can experience the same kind of disorientation when it comes to their company and their brand. You've been so immersed in what you're doing, and you're incredibly invested in both the cause and the outcome. So the exit process—and all the critical evaluation that often comes with that—can be disorienting.

I see it a lot in the B-to-B tech space. An entrepreneur has come up with what he or she genuinely believes is a market-shaking innovation, and the world should be beating down the door. But when the company surrounding that innovation goes under the microscope of a potential acquirer, and the entrepreneur hears a lukewarm report about the prospects of his or her innovation, that can be extremely hard to deal with.

That is completely normal. You're dealing with a negotiation, and many negotiators believe that expressing too much affinity or enthusiasm for a potential purchase means they're essentially negotiating themselves into a higher price.

But there are other important things to remember about

this "disorientation." You need to have a trusted group around you, to provide context and a reality check for the stimuli you're going to be getting during this time. When you have somebody in my seat, as the brand expert, able to use real data and real analysis to show you what your actual market position is—no matter what a hungry acquirer says while trying to get your business for a little cheaper—you can relax a little.

One of the basic things I do with clients on a regular basis is continue to ask the "why" questions and hold up the mirror to what they're doing. Explain to me why this innovation makes better operational sense for your target customer. Tell me why you've been telling this particular kind of story in your branding and marketing over the last 18 months. Remind me what the killer tech is that the other people in your space can't replicate.

Going over that ground repeatedly accomplishes a couple of things. First, it helps us distill the key messaging for the brand that should be a basic part of its DNA. Second, it reinforces to you, the entrepreneur and the leader of the brand, all of the good stuff that put you in a position to potentially exit in the first place.

Understanding not only the value of what you have but what that value could be in the future is a forward-looking skill, and one that you need to bring to the table. A good investment banker will have some sense of that projection, but nobody knows that potential better than the entrepreneur in the main seat. If what you see in that mirror is distorted, the deal you end up with will be distorted, too.

Also, remember this about the exit process as it gets under way: it's okay to say no! It's like a job interview at a company you always imagined would be awesome to work for. It really would be awesome if it was guaranteed that when you scored the interview to finally get to that place, the person doing the interview was perceptive and open, and the job was a perfect match for your skills.

But it doesn't always work that way. And that's okay.

As I said before, sometimes the finances are a fit, but the cultural match just isn't there. Dick Emerson says, "I've been a consultant with a few companies that have gone through this exit process with business brokers, and as the process wore on, you could tell in your heart of hearts that the deal just wasn't a fit. But what makes it so hard is, there's been so much work to get to that place that it is often so tempting to just keep pushing. You've had all this due diligence done and signed all these non-disclosure documents, and you feel like you're exposed and they know everything about you. From that place, it's so easy for the self-loathing to come in, where you're telling yourself if you did a better job, you wouldn't be in this position."

What does a good deal look like?

It depends on your options. It depends on almost everything. If there ever was a situation where you would say "your mileage will vary," it would be that one. All of the variables are the reason a group of seasoned advisors who know all of your relevant facts is so important. But there are certainly some global things that apply to every situation, some hallmarks of deals that have produced satisfying outcomes beyond the dollar amount that appears during the wire transfer.

You want to feel good about what's happening next—whether that's inside the business as somebody assisting an exit, or staying as a part of the new entity, or moving on to the next challenge. You feel good when you've done the branding job properly, taken your shot, and seen the result. Does that mean you can only be happy if you've extracted every dollar and won every deal point? Absolutely not. If you're holding yourself to that standard, you'll probably never actually exit because you won't find terms you can accept; and if you do exit, you'll tear yourself up with regret over failing to meet an impossible standard.

The best exits give you an opportunity to do more of what you enjoy, and take off your plate the things you dislike or aren't as good at. "It's accretive," says Dick. "It's an opportunity, where, if done properly, you're freed to do what you do best. Instead of the HR stuff being on your shoulders, or the finance department stuff being over your head, that goes away and allows you to be a better you."

One of my favorite stories Dick tells is about when he was in charge of multiple divisions at Arnold, and he was interested in learning who in management positions—regardless of whether they were in a creative or more administrative job—were wired for growth, openness, and perceptiveness. He would routinely bring to his review meetings a small bonsai tree for each employee. When he came back for his next circuit six months later, the performers with the most enthusiastic support from their teams (and the highest achievers, regardless of category) were the ones who were attuned to the health of the tree. The ones who let the tree dry out and die were almost always more negative and stuck in what wasn't working, instead of being open and receptive.

Does that mean you have to be a good gardener to be a good entrepreneur? Of course not. But it does mean that finding the space where you can do things you enjoy keeps your channel from being overloaded.

That perspective is especially incisive when it comes to small-shop entrepreneurs who have been filling so many roles themselves during the start-up phase. There's no shame in being a software developer who has no fundamental interest in storytelling (or CRM or the specifics of double-net building leases). This is why you bring in experts to fill in those blanks. Frankly, it's why I built The Grist to operate as a kind of branding quick-reaction force: to come in and help companies do the work they probably don't have the staffing or expertise to accomplish in-house—but do it in a way that matches the agility and energy of a start-up.

How can you efficiently expand your team beyond the walls of your company—and what kinds of questions will those subject-matter experts help you answer? Turn the page and check out Chapter 8.

CHAPTER 8

Disrupting M&A: Are You Ready for the New Player?

Get used to the term M&A. It means "Mergers and Acquisitions," and you'll be seeing more of these M&A specialists as your business piques their interest.

By now, you know I believe in the concept of building brand value in anticipation of and preparation for a buyout. It is my absolute mission and passion to help you get the deal you deserve for the ideas you've developed and work you've put in. The case studies you've read so far have documented what the last decade or so has looked like in this space. Branding your company for buyout is a real thing you need to integrate into your world. If you're not convinced by the success stories of these entrepreneurs, here's one more bit of persuasive evidence.

The fundamental trait every entrepreneur has is courage.

Whether you acknowledge it or not, when you put yourself and your idea out there—when you decide to no longer be an employee in somebody else's dream—you're taking a risk and betting on yourself.

The next fundamental trait an entrepreneur needs is vision. What does the market look like now for what I do or what I sell, and what is it going to be? What does the chess board look like in four moves or ten moves?

How that vision looks to you obviously depends on your particular situation, but the goal in this chapter is to show you some of the emerging trends in the space where the worlds of branding "exit/liquidity" by acquisition or initial public offering meet. I'm going to do it by asking a series of five questions, and offer my take—with the help of some extremely wise and experienced colleagues.

Question 1: What's the difference between a product and a company?

My friend Chris Velis has one of the most interesting jobs on the planet. He's the executive chairman and founder of Miraki Innovation, a Boston-based think tank/venture firm in the medical technology entrepreneurship space. Chris's company looks for opportunities to build start-ups that change the game worldwide for people who are suffering. He helps turn cutting-edge science and research into tools that not only have real-time, real-world applications, but also offer vision that fundamentally changes the game—like Auris Health, the surgical robotics company he started and ultimately sold to Johnson & Johnson for almost $6 billion in 2019.

One of the biggest blind spots he sees in the world of branding is entrepreneurs who think the product they make *is* the company. This is especially true in the world of B-to-B tech, where a feature or innovation can be the main selling point for why a client should be using your solution vs. another competitor's.

Historically, it might have been a way for a traditional consumer products company to talk to its customers. For decades, how did Coca-Cola advertise to you? It put its brand and its colors on everything from race cars to billboards. The product, Coke, *was* the company.

But contrast that approach to what the most resonant brands of today are doing. "Right now, Tesla is valued at more than all the other car companies combined," says Chris. "Why do you think that is? Either everybody who is buying the stock is wrong, or Elon Musk isn't really in the car business. Looking at Tesla a different way, you see that it's an energy company that's in the business of changing logistics, and an energy company that is in the business of changing mobility. A car just happens to be the first product. The brand is far more than just any single product—which makes it so much more valuable."

Apple? Same pattern. "Do you think Steve Jobs started out thinking he was competing with IBM, or do you think he knew from day one he was in the business of making communication and interaction more accessible?" says Chris. "Is Apple a laptop company? A computer company? Or even a phone company?

I'd say, I don't know exactly what they are, but they're wrapped around everything in my life. They're enabling communication beyond any single device or product."

That's the real message for entrepreneurs to take—right from the formation phase, long before you're even thinking about buyouts and exits. "As entrepreneurs and technologists, we didn't truly appreciate what brands were," says Velis. "Especially in tech, entrepreneurs can think of the brand as fluff. But it's not. It's concrete. You build it. You communicate it. Nobody says 'think of your company as the product,' but a company on Wall Street literally *is* a product. Securities in it are bought and sold every single day."

Chris is right: The most successful—and most satisfying—entrepreneurship experiences happen when the brand story is built right from the beginning, as a part of a very specific creation strategy. It comes from asking the right questions.

- What is my mission?
- Why am I trying to accomplish that mission?
- What problem do I want to solve for my customers?
- How am I going to communicate that story?

"To build a company for exit, you not only need to build a product for the customer, but build the company as a product for a customer that is an acquirer," says Velis. "'Either I'm going to go public or sell it' isn't an exit strategy. Who are you going to sell to and why? Where is the puck moving? Where are they going to be in five to seven years? If there are five or six companies like yours, is there room for another one?"

"When you do that, you're starting at a much different place that isn't just about the product," says Velis. "You're engineering the design of your company as thoughtfully as you're designing the products or service you offer. You're creating the opportunity for an exponential difference between the value of the product you sell and the value of your company."

You can see those valuations playing out in real time today, in the home-tech space. An old-fashioned analysis of Nest's smart-thermostat business would examine things like how many potential customers could install a $150 thermostat and connect it to WiFi. But Google understood that a Nest thermostat is really the gateway to a connected home—and all that entails. "If I'm selling Nest devices, is it about how many thermostats I can sell, or is it about being at the forefront of the conscious home? The forefront of health care? The forefront of energy?" asks Velis. "Why did Lululemon buy Mirror for $500 million? Was it to sell more mirrors? Or was it to show you what the newest workout clothes look like, and establish a retail presence right in your house?"

I realize that it isn't necessarily everyone's ambition to build the next Apple or change the world like Chris's latest start-up, which uses filtering technology—originally created to help battle life-threatening sepsis infections in developing countries—to control the spread of COVID-19. But the lessons apply even if scale and a lucrative exit aren't your primary intentions. They get you thinking about the different ways you need to be able to communicate to be not only successful, but viable.

By determining what problems you're going to solve for your customer, you're starting to take control of establishing not only what your customers want and need, but what they'll pay for. You're creating that brand story. "But the way you communicate that to a customer is different than how you'd communicate to a potential acquirer—or to a potential investor," says Velis. "Those are all different audiences, and the messages to each of them are different in their level of complexity. Somebody who wants to invest in a company might not be so concerned about whether strategic synergies exist or not. They want to know what they're going to get out of the investment."

In fact, these factors are the primary reason Velis rarely buys existing companies and instead prefers to build them from scratch himself. "To me, you can't start the process of developing that brand story soon enough, because it sets your course and trajectory," Chris says. "If you don't, you're going to end up in the wrong place and wander around because you didn't set a course for where you wanted to go."

The mission and purpose questions come first in this exercise because they are the heart and soul of what you're doing. They're the *why*—why you put in all the hours and the sweat and the commitment and the intensity in the first place. "One of the problems I see with entrepreneurs and folks on Wall Street is that they think there's a cheap way out," says Velis. "They think it's about simply looking at some numbers on a piece of paper. But the dollars are always going to be compromised if you don't aspire to higher values, like discipline and integrity and sense of purpose. And when you deal with those things on the front end and truly commit to them, then you can communicate the brand effectively. When you can't look inside and authoritatively say, 'This is what we're all about—and our mission is to go to the moon,' the banker shows up at the end and sells you as a revenue stream or an income statement.

"A big company might hire a consultant like McKinsey to come in and tell them that nobody cares about what they're doing anymore—and that they better start caring about what customers care about or they won't be in business," says Velis. "But a company has to find its own soul. If you're asking somebody to come in and find your soul, you're in trouble. But if you have somebody like Ted come in and help the discussions about how best to talk about it to all those different audiences—from the day-to-day customers to potential acquirers—that's using it for the best purpose. Somebody needs to be integrated in the process who knows how to communicate what a company is. It's such a dynamic thing."

Every month, I get calls from potential clients who essentially want me to come in to manufacture this "soul" Chris has been describing to help reposition a product, revive a brand, or get a company ready to be put on the market. Those aren't projects I tend to take. It's far more satisfying for me (and I expect it would be for you) to reveal the soul that is already in your story, and that has been built into it from the start—even if that work requires some archaeological digging, so to speak.

Question 2: How will entrepreneurship education evolve?

Boston might be the best place in the world to study business, with Harvard, MIT, Boston University, Boston College, and Babson all within a 20-square-mile area. Harvard gets a lot of attention, and deservedly so, but Babson's entrepreneurship program is widely acclaimed, to the point that *U.S. News and World Report* has named it the best in the world 28 years in a row.

The folks at Babson have always been great to me, and the school has been an important avenue for testing and validating concepts. After working on Branding For Buyout for a few years, I had the opportunity to be a part of a case study for one of Babson's entrepreneurship classes. I was curious to see what conclusions students came to after they had a chance to do some research. I was hoping to get a credible outside opinion that would add more validation to my thesis—that Branding For Buyout could be a standalone business, and it could disrupt the mergers-and-acquisitions marketplace.

The six-member team of rising-star international students assigned to my case was led by Amir Abedrabo and mentored by lecturer Dwight Gertz—who was a partner at Bain & Company and the president of Celerant Americas. They came to several conclusions that remain cornerstones of my business today: Yes, Branding For Buyout is disruptive to the M&A space, and it's an opportunity to partner with investment banks to reveal full value for early-stage and mature entrepreneurial businesses at exit.

Some of my favorite experiences have been guest lecturing in Babson classes taught by my friends Dr. Andrew Corbett and Dr. Candy Brush. Dr. Corbett is the Paul T. Babson Distinguished Professor of Entrepreneurial Studies, and he's been called one of the top 25 entrepreneurship researchers in the world by the *Journal of Business Management.* Dr. Brush—who you'll hear more from in the next section—is the F.W. Olin Distinguished Professor of Entrepreneurship, and co-founder of the Diana International Project, a group of 600 researchers worldwide committed to expanding female entrepreneurship.

I think all of us share the same sense of excitement about the frontier that is Branding For Buyout. As Dr. Corbett says, "Even savvy business students and talented young entrepreneurs don't realize that the day you decide to take professional investment is the day you've decided to sell your company. There's no other way for those investors to get their money back unless there's some sort of exit. Bankers own that exit process, and they generally do a good job, but they're showing the asset—your business—through a very specific financial light. What Ted is doing is something that can have an industry built around it—a better way for people who are looking for an exit to emphasize and enhance the overall value of their asset, as opposed to just the financial piece. That's new territory, and exciting ground to cover."

Babson's program is composed of more than 30 different courses on specific pieces of entrepreneurship, covering everything from franchising to running a family business to understanding how to identify and buy a promising small business. Until now, most of the academic coverage about exits was seen through mergers and acquisitions—but even that was geared more toward the acquirer than the seller. "At Babson, we're focused on getting entrepreneurial leaders who are trying to find a business to actually start one—iterate through ideas and market incubations to see what's right," says Dr. Corbett. "You're so far away from exit at that point, but still, if people are investing in you, you're going to have to sell it. Nobody has been teaching that in a real, methodical way."

Given what Chris Velis has to say about the importance of making your start-up attractive to acquirers right from the start, it's clear that the time to teach exit skills to entrepreneurial students is now. They actually need those skills *before they start a company,* not just when they're getting ready to sell it.

"I was just having this conversation a few weeks ago with a friend and former student who sold his company to a private-equity firm," recalls Dr. Corbett. "The venture development people are expecting him to build this business, but they also see a place for the base technology to go in another direction. That wasn't what was negotiated in the deal, and he's having a really hard time with it. Most entrepreneurs get good at the exit the *second* time they do it. The goal is to give people some tools to do it right the first time."

Reviewing financials and performing data analysis will always be part of a business school's curriculum, but top schools like Babson spend comparatively more time on teaching skills that are much harder to commoditize. "Human decision makers are much better than machines at some things, while machines are better at doing things like predicting through artificial intelligence and machine learning," says Dr. Corbett. "Finance folks deal more with predictive, algorithmic things than the branding part. We still have preferences, and humans are still the arbiters of what they prefer."

Of course, the ultimate "dirty little secret" about the last 50 years of mergers and acquisitions driven primarily by investment bankers is that the track record for those deals isn't particularly good. Some 85 percent of acquisitions, historically, *don't* produce the returns projected in advance of the deal—and a 2011 *Harvard Business Review* study concluded that between 70 and 90 percent of mergers fail outright. "It costs a lot more money to bring companies together," Corbett says. "Instead of talking about finances, you could be getting an acquirer to focus on the future with the possibilities of what the asset could be. And that's where I see new opportunities. Marketing used to be the place where they put the creative folks who were afraid of numbers. But marketing is becoming more of a science than an art, because it's so dependent on data. The entrepreneurs who get savvy about the technology and the science behind it, but are still able to tell the story, are going to win the day going forward."

Question 3: How does a non-traditional entrepreneur survive and thrive?

If what Dr. Corbett says is true—that 85 percent of

acquisitions don't live up to the expectations of the acquirer—what does that tell you about the way acquisitions are approached, researched, and closed?

It should tell you that we need to do a much better job at all of those phases—both as entrepreneurs and within the mergers-and-acquisitions space altogether.

Dr. Candy Brush is doing just that, both in her role as a professor of entrepreneurship at Babson and a researcher investigating the roadblocks women face in entrepreneurship and devising paths over, around, and through them.

If you're an entrepreneur who didn't have the head-start of being educated at a prestigious school, and was never part of the inner circle shared by people with similar backgrounds, you're not alone. Whether you're a woman, a person of color, or a blue-collar worker in Middle America, you don't have the same resources available to you as somebody who came from an Ivy League environment (or Stanford, or Babson, or any other school with a strong reputation and network of graduates).

So how does that change the way you need to operate?

The good news is that the democratization of technology has made it easier than ever to *start* a business. "All you need is a cell phone and a computer, and you can easily start a business for less than $5,000," says Dr. Brush. "There are also more resources for women entrepreneurs than there were even 10 years ago in terms of networking, Small Business Association funding, and Department of Labor resources that are directed toward women [and people of color]."

Technical horsepower is available to small businesses in the simple form of, say, an iPhone—which an entrepreneur can use to take high-definition photos and videos, upload them to a website-building program, and connect to a credit-card processing service like Stripe to collect payments in real time. Sole proprietors can stay agile and keep costs low, compared to their larger competitors.

Dr. Brush runs a program out of Babson that mentors female-owned micro-businesses—ones that have less than $200,000 in sales per year—and even during the pandemic-ravaged 2020, only three of the 38 businesses closed, while nine had record-setting sales. "Regardless of the kind of company you are, the ability to quickly pivot is so important," says Brush. "If you're a single-product business, and you could convert to delivery during the pandemic—for example, having access to mentorship while having a crisis like this happen—if you could pull yourself through it, you can probably do anything."

Where the picture gets cloudier is when it comes to growing. Entrepreneurs who want to expand will need networks, and they need capital. Let's say you're a female entrepreneur who runs a small B-to-B healthcare company, with a technological innovation that could change the way people are treated in the home. If you're interested in extending your reach beyond your local market, what are your options? You might find an angel investor—someone from your local market who has a personal interest in seeing you succeed, or one of the angel investment organizations dedicated to funding good ideas from underrepresented groups within your specific business category. Brush says about 30 percent of angel capital is going to female-led start-ups.

That's encouraging, but it also casts a negative light on what's happening in the world of venture capital. Dr. Brush was a part of a research group that examined 30 years of institutional venture-capital funding in the United States and found that only 15 percent of companies with such funding had even one woman on their leadership teams, while about three percent went to companies with female founders. The numbers for African Americans and Hispanics are even bleaker, at less than a tenth of one percent.

Institutional venture-capital groups that have a female partner are 40 percent more likely to invest in a company with a woman CEO, but 92 percent of VC partners are male. "To me, it signals that the business of funding companies is broken," says Dr. Brush. "Since VCs make their money on management fees, the only way the industry is going to change is when limited partners put pressure on the firms and say, I don't want my dollars going to a limited percentage of the population. I want it to reach the entire qualified population."

One of the strengths of an education at a place like Babson is that it not only provides students with the tools they need to start a business, but it also leaves them with built-in networks of mentors who have walked the same road. For entrepreneurs coming from outside that ecosystem, that means spending time and energy to try to replicate some of that networking. Luckily, that's becoming easier and easier to do.

One of Dr. Brush's favorite examples is run by the James Beard Foundation—a group dedicated to promoting fine food and the artistry of preparing it. Dr. Brush and the foundation work with female chefs and restaurant owners who have achieved some level of success, to help them jump from local to regional, and regional to national. "Some of the women in the program want to scale what they have, and some of them want to build it so they can sell it," Dr. Brush says. "They all have different goals and big business ideas. We pair them with mentors who can help them navigate all the aspects that go beyond preparing the food—mentors who have already sold restaurants and have already grown and expanded. They get a lot of role models."

That concept of role modeling is a huge one for *any* entrepreneur, but it's especially true for founders who haven't been exposed to many possibilities. When you can see the path somebody else has taken with a product like yours or a process in a similar category, it's easier to imagine that it can happen—and at least give you the chance to ask the right questions!

"Just getting to the point of knowing there's something there you don't know about and need to learn is a big, big step," says Dr. Brush. "It gives you an awareness that there's something out there you should be considering. In our small start-up program, we ask the enrollees, what do you want this to be in five years? Do you want to own it? Do you want to grow it and sell it? Having that mindset guides where you put your attention and helps prioritize the decisions you make."

Question 4: What kind of human skills will entrepreneurs need?

A few years ago, I was in a bad place. The agency I ran had become a part of a bigger group, and I had gone from being an owner back to being an employee. I knew what I wanted to do, which was to get out and go back to the agency side on my own again, and mature Branding For Buyout full time. It all manifested itself in this sharp pain behind my left shoulder blade—which I always get when I'm stressed out. My speaking voice had become higher and tighter, I wasn't sleeping, and I was just miserable.

I put in a call to Dan Guglielmo, the executive coach I had been working with for about a year. Dan has worked with a wide variety of CEOs in tech, finance, and marketing in the Boston area, and he's been a successful entrepreneur in his own right as the founder of the Exit Planning Exchange—an association of advisors who work with private business owners, all the way from founding to exit and on to estate planning.

What came next wasn't some kind of pep talk you'd see in a movie or at halftime of a college football game. What Dan does is help entrepreneurs recognize and deal with the emotions they're experiencing in a productive way—instead of either burying them or letting them turn into non-productive behavior that gets in the way of progress.

He asked me to walk into an empty conference room and look out the window at the blue sky, to change my perspective. I told him I felt like Atlas, with the pressure of the world on my shoulders. If I jumped back into the world of entrepreneurship, what would that potentially mean for me and my family? Was it a risk I should even consider taking?

I was freaking out, but Dan didn't tell me to ignore my fear. He had me lean into the pain and the suffering. He wanted me to feel it, and examine it. "The Buddhists say, whenever you meet fear, just be with it. Don't go this way or that way. And it will disappear," Dan says. "Just by being with your pain, you'll feel a shift in energy."

For me, when I went through my worst-case scenarios, I was able to see that I was still okay. I was still there. My breathing changed, and my voice went back down to its normal pitch. I could see the possibilities that were hidden by the fear.

"When a leader comes to me, there's usually some angst there because of how much is tied up in the decisions he or she has to make," Dan says. "And they come thinking they have to learn how to do something, to take care of the company to make things 'better.' But what I'm interested in doing is helping them manage their anxiety to make *them* better. Let's get you to the space you need to be, because you already know the answers. You just need to have the space to be yourself."

I realize that might sound "syrupy" for some of the hard-core tech types reading this book. Things like feelings and emotions aren't a part of performance or building a brand, right? The truth is that most entrepreneurs are specialized high achievers already. They know a huge amount about the space they're in. They're smart, motivated people.

The issue isn't smarts, or information.

It's doing a better job handling the emotions that come with being human. When you can handle those emotions better yourself, you can do a better job handling the things that come your way, both as the decision maker in a company and as a father, mother, friend, or colleague.

There isn't enough room in this book to go into a full description of the tools somebody like Dan uses to help somebody develop more awareness. The point of this chapter is to show you a space you might not have considered before.

Consider how our brains and senses actually work. "Your subconscious mind is 3,000 times faster than your ability to cognitively process information," Dan says. "So when something is happening out there, you're first feeling it as energy in the moment. The clients who come to me are cognitively smart. They don't need me to help them get sharper. What they need me to do is help them get out of their heads. To drop into their bodies and use the whole body as a brain. What is my present state? Am I nervous? Am I angry? Am I frustrated? Am I shrinking or expanding? When you can see and feel the space between an event and your reaction to it, you can respond in the way that creates the reality you want."

In the moment, the answer isn't *more* information or thinking *harder*. It's being more present and aware of how you feel, and making intentional decisions. What does that look like in practice? In our own work, Dan and I use waves as metaphors all the time—like sets of waves coming in. What I've learned is that the waves never stop coming. I used to operate under the philosophy that anything was possible in 90 days—and I would burn myself out as hard as I could to make it happen. I still believe that you can get something huge done in that time, but I also know now that while energy is a strength, you have to be able to regulate it. You have to learn when to take care of yourself and take the day off. You have to know which waves to ride and which to duck. If you keep trying to ride every wave, you're going to get pounded back into the reef, and you'll be out of commission for a month.

Like I said, the concepts of coaching and self-development are so rich that they could be the subjects of their own complete books. Two small samples from my own journey would be, first, take some time between action and reaction; and second, be aware that there are always new things to learn.

"The growth mindset is a form of humility," says Dan. "It says, I've been wrong before, and I could be wrong again. I've got a lot to learn, and I'm a lifetime learner. That's humility, and that's a prerequisite to perform well with coaching. If you have the humility and desire, you absolutely can transform yourself."

Question 5: Where does Branding For Buyout fit?

From everything you've heard from the people in this chapter, it's obvious there are some flaws and limitations in the old world of exits. I trademarked the terminology for Branding For Buyout back in 2012, because I firmly believed there was a huge opportunity to add value within the mergers-and-acquisitions space. So much of the business has become big data and analytics and number crunching.

Don't get me wrong. The math matters, and there are a lot of shrewd operators out there—in private equity, in venture capital, in tech, and in the spectrum of other forward-looking categories. They know how to identify opportunities—in the form of entrepreneurs and start-ups who are doing cutting-edge things, and in the shape of small companies with assets that aren't being used enough.

But the value of your vision is more than that. And Branding For Buyout is an opportunity to tell that story.

It's a way for everybody to win. If you're the entrepreneur, the risk-taker, the person who built this thing from the ground up, Branding For Buyout is one of the tools you have to have to make sure your creation gets its full value in a sale. If you're the investment banker trying to put together a seller and a buyer, Branding For Buyout helps you tell the fully developed story of both product and company. You have a better product to sell, and to place with a buyer. If you're the buyer, Branding For Buyout does the crucial brand development work you will be (or *should* be) doing to enhance what you bought, and offers a roadmap for growth.

If Google or Facebook or Ford or Johnson & Johnson came to you right now to buy your start-up, who would you need to have at the table to pull off the deal? There's the investment banker who helped orchestrate the courtship. Lawyers and accountants must always be involved to make sure the bases are covered and the numbers are validated. Also, you'll probably need an expert to help you direct where the proceeds of the sale will go—for tax, investment, and legacy considerations.

Your brand has to have a seat at the table, and that seat comes in the form of Branding For Buyout.

The techniques in this book have been battle tested and proven to create momentum, generate excitement, and—most importantly—offer direction to a brand and make it not only more attractive to a buyer, but translate into a more lucrative sale.

What kinds of things can stand in the way?

What I'm about to say will be familiar to subject-matter experts. If you're the go-to person on the planet for, say, delivering massive digital files efficiently through the cloud, you're going to tune out if somebody with no credentials tries to tell you about the intricate technical details of your business. You're confident that you know better. On the other hand, if you've spent the last decade in the trenches coming up with genius-level tech, making it easy for pop stars to record tracks with producers and performers simultaneously across five different studios around the world, are you confident you know how to tell that brand story *and* sell your company for the highest return?

I know the answer, because I've sold a couple of my own companies early on and not gotten what I hoped, and I've consulted with companies (as you've read) that have done it right. As it stands, that process is dominated by the investment banker. That has some procedural advantages, but also some caveats—like selling your house through a realtor.

Ultimately, investment bankers are driven to close deals,

and close them quickly. That's how they get paid, and that's what frees them to move onto the next deal. For a good investment banker, that means a lifetime of deals. But if you're an entrepreneur sitting in the sweet spot, with an idea and a company and brand that could change the world, you're setting up to do your one deal of a lifetime. That means you and the banker shepherding the deal have *some* common interests, but not all of them line up perfectly.

To get the full value for what you're building, it's up to you to build it with every tool at your disposal. It's *your* dream.

With Branding For Buyout, there's finally a playbook you can follow to reveal and extract that value.

I'm intentionally using the word "extract," because it's just like what goes on at a mine. You have to do some digging. The work I've described in this book isn't some paint-by-numbers project you can finish in a few hours with a Squarespace account and a crowd-sourced mission statement.

It takes the average chief executive 18 to 24 months to properly prepare a company for exit. It takes time, expertise and, yes, money to do it correctly. Entrepreneurs can (and do) wing it and hope for the best, and they almost always leave money on the table. Lots of it—and, sometimes, *all of it.* And before you go pointing to some mad genius who sold a company for a billion dollars and retired to a beach somewhere, imagine your chances of winning the lottery, and ask yourself if this is actually a sound business model!

Like anything else done correctly, a successful exit requires preparation, research, perseverance, hard work, and vision. The most successful entrepreneurs see the variables that move the needle most, and that's where they concentrate their attention. As Chris Velis says, they "begin with the end in mind."

What does that end look like for you? We're in the middle of a literal tsunami of innovation, entrepreneurism, and mergers-and-acquisitions activity. You can feel the push to learn more, move faster, and advance the life cycle of your company into maturity.

Remember the lessons from the cases in this book—you'll need them to avoid the biggest traps. The energy you need is already there. You can harness that energy and make your plan work.

Are you ready?

Thank You

This is my first book, and it took a village. The idea for Branding For Buyout spans almost 15 years of effort from concept to commercialization. It's been a labor of love that has demanded grit and tenacity. I never even thought about wavering because of the people around me. You were there when I needed you most—and for that, I'm eternally grateful. There are too many people to call you all out individually, but I'll do the best I can. The circle around me is gratifyingly large.

To my family, I'm so grateful for your perseverance. To my friends, thank you for your neverending belief and support. My team at The Grist? You're the best I've ever worked with. The original Crunch crew, the Breakaway crew, the Wasabi start-up crew—so many great memories and experiences.

This book wouldn't be what it is without the generosity of the interview subjects. Tom Seeman, Paul Nardone, Karen Pitts, David Friend, Dr. Andrew Corbett, Dr. Candy Brush, Mike Torto, Mike Welts, Chris Velis, Joe Moriarty, Meredith McPherron, Gary Cormier, Deb Besemer, Amir Abedrabo, and Ameen Amin—many thanks for your time, wisdom, and observations.

To my literary agent, Maura Phelan, who championed me and this idea from the beginning. To my Branding For Buyout CMO Alex Proelss for "compartmentalizing." To my coach, Dan Guglielmo, who helped me see and ride wave after wave. Special thanks to Scott MacGillivray for proofreading. And finally, to my content engine, Matt Rudy. If you want to bring an idea to life and write a book, he's your guy.

Glossary

B-to-B

Abbreviation for business-to-business, it means a company concentrates its development, branding, marketing, and sales efforts with other companies, not with individual consumers. For example, a company that sells enterprise cloud storage to international companies or electric seat motors to car manufacturers is in the B-to-B space. Also written as B2B.

B-to-C

Abbreviation for business-to-consumer, it signifies a company that sells a product or service directly to consumers. For example, if you're an Internet retailer that sells shoes or shirts via your own website (instead of selling them wholesale to another retailer), you're a B-to-C business. Also written as B2C.

B4B

Abbreviation for Branding For Buyout—the book you're reading now. It's a term I trademarked to represent the concept of building a branding strategy specifically for exit.

BFY

Abbreviation for better-for-you, a food category that includes healthy, reduced-, low-, and no-calorie options.

Brand position

Where a brand sits relative to others in the same and adjacent spaces. For example, a competitor to Tesla might want to position itself as a lower-cost alternative with technology that is almost as good, and offer more available colors.

Brand story

The narrative that helps customers understand both why they should buy from you and why they should care about you. It can encompass details about the products and services you offer, the history and innovation behind them, and the problems you want to help the potential customer solve. Apple is an example of a highly developed brand story. You can learn about the features and benefits in a new iPhone, but the overarching story is that Apple makes beautiful, easy-to-use things that make your life easier. It inspires passionate loyalty among its customers.

Branding intent

Defining a future ideal state of a brand, and developing or

framing it relative to that state. For example, if a company wanted to make itself attractive to an international buyer, it would make its established position in the American market (and potential shortcut to multinational growth) a part of its branding intent.

Category

The space you compete in. Understanding your category narrowly means you know who your closest competitors are—and the companies you aspire to compete with. More broadly, it's the space where you could conceivably find an acquirer. A company that sells motorcycle insurance is in a specific category. It could also be acquired by a larger insurance organization that doesn't yet provide motorcycle insurance, and wants an easier entry into that category of insurance.

CIM (Confidential Information Memorandum)

The baseline document an investment banker uses to summarize a company that is for sale. Think of it as the listing if your home went on the market. Good CIMs are effective at both framing a company's financial performance and telling the brand story. Bad ones just repeat dry financial data.

C-level executive

An executive who runs a line of business in a company. A chief, who reports directly to a company head. C-level executives include the CEO (chief executive officer), CFO (chief financial officer), CTO (chief technical officer), and CMO (chief marketing officer).

Cloud storage

Data that does not reside inside the computer on your desk (or on your phone) but is quickly retrievable from another place on a network. For example, a company might produce digital video advertisements from multiple locations. The video files could be stored on central servers and moved to local computers if a particular employee needed to work on them.

Dev

Short for "developer" or "development." For example, a web-dev company is one that conceives and builds websites for clients.

EPA

Abbreviation for the Environmental Protection Agency—a federal department in charge of setting and enforcing rules concerning water, air, and toxic substances.

IDC

Abbreviation for the International Data Corporation, a leading market research and intelligence company in the IT, telecommunications, and consumer tech categories.

Investment banker

The person who scouts, vets, and advises companies and aligns them for a potential sale or purchase. For example, an investment banker with experience and contacts in the home health care space would presumably know what the potential market is for a start-up, and orchestrate the sale of the start-up to a larger player.

M&A

Abbreviation for mergers and acquisitions. Bankers, lawyers, accountants, and brand developers who specialize in preparing companies to be bought or sold work in the M&A space.

Platform

A collection of organized products and services from a company that provides a common starting point or connection point for other users. Amazon is a platform that sellers use to find customers, feature products, and conduct transactions. Buyers find products, pay for them, and arrange for them to be shipped in one place—on the platform.

Playbook

A specific set of processes, procedures, rules, and best practices. Ideally, a new hire would be able to follow a playbook and come up to speed quickly.

Scalability

The ability for an organization, brand, or product to expand. A scalable business is one that, with added investment and infrastructure, could grow exponentially. A non-scalable business might be one that relies on the specific, individualized contribution of a person or small team.

Venture capital

A type of financing entrepreneurs often seek to grow or sell their company. A venture-capital firm amasses capital from investors and seeks out companies in early stages that show the potential for explosive growth. The venture-capital firm provides capital in exchange for equity.

Index

Notes

About the Author

Ted Schlueter is an award-winning, brand-building entrepreneur. He's the Founder and CEO of The Grist, a Boston-based brand and marketing agency, and is a pioneer in the world of pre-exit branding. Ted created, developed, and refined the Branding For Buyout method over two decades and used it successfully on high-profile exits including Pop-Corners to PepsiCo and Embotics to Swedish software enterprise, Snow.

Prior to selling his first agency and before launching the Grist, Ted worked in Boston and New York at Arnold Worldwide, Digitas, and Greco Ethridge Group in various leadership roles. When he's not guest lecturing at Babson College or speaking at entrepreneur-focused engagements, Ted is an avid cyclist, an ardent adventurer, and a dedicated family man in Marblehead, Massachusetts.

Additional Resources

Visit brandingforbuyout.com to explore how the B4B methodology has created exponential value for entrepreneurs of all shapes and sizes. CEO testimonials will demystify the process and you'll find more guidance on how to unlock your business's full potential. You can also sign up for our newsletter to receive new research, case studies, and insights from other entrepreneurs and CEOs.

If you're looking for something more customized, or are interested in booking Ted Schlueter for an appearance or speaking engagement, please email PR@brandingforbuyout.com.